Stanley Cavell

AND LITERARY

SKEPTICISM

MICHAEL FISCHER

STANLEY CAVELL
AND
LITERARY SKEPTICISM

Stanley Cavell
and
Literary Skepticism

MICHAEL FISCHER

The University of Chicago Press

Chicago and London

M I C H A E L   F I S C H E R is professor of English at the University
of New Mexico. He is the author of *Does Deconstruction Make Any
Difference?: Poststructuralism and the Defense of Poetry in Modern
Criticism* and coeditor of *Romanticism and Contemporary Criticism*.

The University of Chicago Press, Chicago 60637
The University of Chicago Press, Ltd., London
© 1989 by The University of Chicago
All rights reserved. Published 1989
Printed in the United States of America

98 97 96 95 94 93 92 91 90 89   5 4 3 2 1

Library of Congress Cataloging-in-Publication Data

Fischer, Michael, 1949–
    Stanley Cavell and literary skepticism / Michael Fischer.
      p. cm.
    Includes bibliographies and index.
    ISBN 0–226–25140–3 (alk. paper). — ISBN 0–226–25141–1 (pbk.:
alk. paper)
    1. Literature—Philosophy. 2. Criticism. 3. Cavell, Stanley,
1926– . 4. Skepticism. I. Title.
    PN49.F57 1989
    801—dc19   88–30312
                                              CIP

FOR STANLEY CAVELL

CONTENTS

Abbreviations

Books by Stanley Cavell:

MWM   *Must We Mean What We Say?* 1969. Reprint. Cambridge: Cambridge University Press, 1979.

WV   *The World Viewed.* Enl. ed. 1971. Reprint. Cambridge: Harvard University Press, 1979.

SW   *The Senses of Walden.* Exp. ed. 1972. Reprint. San Francisco: North Point Press, 1981.

CR   *The Claim of Reason.* Oxford: Oxford University Press, 1979.

PH   *Pursuits of Happiness.* Cambridge: Harvard University Press, 1981.

TS   *Themes out of School.* San Francisco: North Point Press, 1984.

DK   *Disowning Knowledge in Six Plays of Shakespeare.* Cambridge: Cambridge University Press, 1987.

Articles by Stanley Cavell:

GRK   "Genteel Responses to Kant? In Emerson's 'Fate' and Coleridge's *Biographia Literaria.*" *Raritan* 3 (Fall 1983): 34–61.

WPT   "What Photography Calls Thinking." *Raritan* 4 (Spring 1985): 1–21.

DT   "The Division of Talent." *Critical Inquiry* 11 (June 1985): 519–38.

IQO   "In Quest of the Ordinary: Texts of Recovery." In *Romanticism and Contemporary Criticism,* ed. Morris Eaves and Michael Fischer. Ithaca: Cornell University Press, 1986.

BOGE   "Being Odd, Getting Even." In *Reconstructing Indi-*

vidualism, ed. Thomas C. Heller et al. Stanford: Stanford University Press, 1986.

PC   "Psychoanalysis and Cinema." In *Images in Our Souls: Cavell, Psychoanalysis, and Cinema*, ed. Joseph H. Smith and William Kerrigan. Baltimore: Johns Hopkins University Press, 1987.

UNPUBLISHED PAPERS OF
STANLEY CAVELL:

BD   "The Melodrama of the Unknown Woman: Bette Davis and *Now Voyager*."

MUW   "The Melodrama of the Unknown Woman: A Reading of *Gaslight*."

PAL   "The Philosopher in American Life."

PME   "Philosophy and the Myth of the Everyday."

UO   "The Uncanniness of the Ordinary."

WPC   "Wittgenstein as a Philosopher of Culture."

PREFACE

STANLEY CAVELL'S WRITINGS range widely over
film, philosophy, literature, literary criticism, painting, music, and even television. One constant in his multifaceted
work, however, is his concern with skepticism. By skepticism
Cavell means the radical epistemological questioning en-
gaged in by René Descartes, David Hume, and others—questioning that leads these philosophers to doubt whether we
can know with certainty the existence of objects and other
minds. Following J. L. Austin, Wittgenstein, and several
literary figures (among them Thoreau and Shakespeare),
Cavell tries not to refute skepticism but to characterize it as
a significant human possibility or temptation.

Cavell's analysis of skepticism offers many things to literary critics: innovative readings of particular works by
Thoreau, Emerson, Poe, Coleridge, Wordsworth, and
Shakespeare, among many others; provocative discussions
of central issues in aesthetics, including the legitimacy of
paraphrase, the function of tragedy, and the definition of
genres; and seminal descriptions of such literary move-
ments as Romanticism and modernism. I focus here,
however, on Cavell's relevance to the controversy still surrounding poststructuralist literary theory, in particular the
work of Jacques Derrida, J. Hillis Miller, Paul de Man, and
Stanley Fish. Although apparently dead or at least dormant
as the subject of polemical debate, "deconstruction" (to use
an admittedly inadequate term) survives as an important
contribution to contemporary thinking about literature.

My interest in starting a discussion of Cavell's work rests
on two assumptions that I will be spending much of this
book trying to support: first, that there are significant affinities between deconstruction and the epistemological skepticism that concerns Cavell, and, secondly, that Cavell's

powerful analysis of Descartes and Hume accordingly permits a fresh view of de Man, Fish, and Derrida. By a fresh view, I do not mean a final solution to some of the questions raised by these theorists. I am using Cavell not to bury deconstruction but to characterize it, even to show why some attacks against it have neither ceased nor worked. I am writing this book for a literary audience that will be approaching Cavell (many for the first time) via literary theory, not philosophy, say, or film. I accordingly present Cavell's work by way of the issues in literary theory that I think it illuminates.

In addition to introducing Cavell's writings, chapter 1 poses the problem of his neglect by many contemporary literary theorists. Despite Cavell's longstanding indebtedness to literature, not very much has been written about him. (This, in fact, is the first book-length discussion of his work.) My first chapter explores the relative lack of attention paid to Cavell by literary theorists—relative, that is, to the considerable interest in another philosopher, Derrida.

Chapter 2 cites some parallels between deconstruction and external-world skepticism, as represented by Cavell. Chapter 3 continues along similar lines, this time relating recent theory to other-minds skepticism, again as characterized by Cavell. Chapter 4 follows Cavell's lead in examining how different genres work out some of the problems raised by skepticism—problems that I have tried to bring up in the preceding two chapters. Chapter 5 uses *The Senses of Walden* and some of Cavell's other writings to show how Cavell draws on American and English Romanticism in fashioning the response to skepticism that I have been describing. Finally, chapter 6 looks at Cavell's "The Politics of Interpretation," "The Division of Talent," and a few other recent essays that specifically refer to de Man, Fish, and other literary theorists. I save these essays for my last chapter because in my view their full impact depends on the treatment of skepticism that I have been trying to sketch.

Using Cavell to characterize deconstruction has meant placing deconstruction in the extraordinary context in which Cavell places skepticism—a context that includes American movies, modernist paintings, and several plays by Shakespeare. If nothing else, this is the first book to associate de Man with Othello and Derrida with Clark Gable (in *It Happened One Night*). I will have succeeded if the reader not only sees the justice of these comparisons but understands that far from belittling recent theory they show my respect for it.

An early version of chapter 2 appeared in *Bucknell Review* 32, no. 1 (1988) as "Stanley Cavell and Contemporary Literary Theory." An early version of chapter 5 appeared in *Soundings* 68 (Fall 1985): 388–403, as "Speech and Writing in *The Senses of Walden*." I thank the editors of these journals for permission to reprint parts of these essays. The following articles by Cavell have been recently published by the University of Chicago Press: "The Philosopher in American Life" and "The Uncanniness of the Ordinary" (in *In Quest of the Ordinary: Lines of Skepticism and Romanticism* [1989]) and "Wittgenstein as a Philosopher of Culture" (in *This New Yet Unapproachable America* [1989]). These publications appeared after my own book had gone to press.

Finishing this book gives me the chance to thank some of the people who have helped me with it. In revising the book, I benefited from an especially challenging and attentive reader's report by Richard Wheeler. I am also deeply indebted to Gus Blaisdell, not only for introducing me to Cavell's work but for keeping me in touch with it. I have dedicated the book to Stanley Cavell. His encouragement got me started; his example and guidance kept me going. The support of my wife, Kim, has been crucial to my own pursuit of happiness, not to mention my finishing this project. Finally, I want to mention my children, Joshua and Sarah. They were not simply on my mind when I wrote this book; they were often in the same room. I want to thank them for being there—and for occasionally leaving.

1

STANLEY CAVELL
AND CONTEMPORARY
LITERARY THEORY

STANLEY CAVELL AND Literary Skepticism brings together two sets of texts that have thus far barely touched: Stanley Cavell's work on skepticism and the recent writings of Paul de Man, J. Hillis Miller, Stanley Fish, Jacques Derrida, and other poststructuralist critics. My attention to Cavell rests on two assumptions already mentioned in the Preface: first, that there are important affinities between poststructuralist criticism and the epistemological skepticism that concerns Cavell, and, secondly, that Cavell's analysis of skepticism makes available a fresh approach to deconstruction and other tendencies in contemporary literary theory.

I say that Cavell's writings and contemporary theory have barely touched in part because Cavell's remarks on recent criticism are scattered and provisional, pointing to a path not (yet) taken by his own work. He first alludes to deconstruction in his preface to *The Senses of Walden* (1972), a book that discusses, among other things, Thoreau's commitment to writing (as opposed to speech). Noting that he has been asked to relate Thoreau on this point to Derrida and Lévi-Strauss, Cavell replies, "I do not yet know or understand the pertinent views of these authors well enough to dispute or agree with them" (SW, xiv).[1] In his 1978 foreword to *The Claim of Reason*, Cavell cites recent unspecified developments in French thought and their enthusiastic reception by American literary critics but still says, "I am not, not at any rate here and now, prepared to speak to this" (CR, xiv). Even more recently, in "The Politics of Interpretation," Cavell's contribution to a 1981 *Critical Inquiry* symposium, he admits that his "ambivalence" toward recent developments in literary theory has made it difficult for him to study them "in any very orderly way." In part because of his interest "in

1

the possibility of art as a possibility of knowing, or acknowledging" (TS, 48), Cavell seems uneasy with deconstruction
but still disavows any intention "of providing a 'reading
of [it]' " (TS, 58). He approaches deconstruction cautiously,
neither spurning nor embracing it: "If deconstruction, as
in de Man's recommendation of it, is to disillusion us,
it is a noble promise and to be given welcome. Disillusion
is what fits us for reality, whether in Plato's terms or
D. W. Winnicott's. But then we must be assured that this
promise is based on a true knowledge of what our illusions
are" (TS, 55).

Cavell's reluctance to say much about deconstruction—
one of the most important (certainly one of the most
discussed) developments in literary theory since the New
Criticism—perhaps has contributed to his neglect by American literary theorists. The handful of theorists who have
commented on him typically praise him and lament his neglect without, however, doing much to remedy it.[2] In *Criticism in the Wilderness*, Geoffrey Hartman, for example, calls
The Senses of Walden "essential for anyone interested in the
possibility of a philosophical criticism of literature."[3] But he
pays this compliment in a footnote to a book that includes
extensive commentary on several philosophers. Very little
has been written on Cavell, especially in comparison to the
flood of publications on Derrida—no books, only a few articles, and a smattering of serious reviews.

The literary underpinnings of Cavell's work make his neglect by critical theorists more surprising than it may first
appear. The author of books on *Walden*, the theory of film,
and Hollywood film comedy, Cavell has also written at
length on *Coriolanus*, *King Lear*, various essays by Emerson,
the "Intimations" Ode, *The Rime of the Ancient Mariner*, *Endgame*, contemporary music, modernist painting, some short
stories by Poe, and television. Even *The Claim of Reason*, Cavell's most formidably philosophical work, is studded with
references to literary texts and concludes with a reading of
The Merchant of Venice, *The Winter's Tale*, and *Othello*. As
I will be showing, these excursions into the arts, especially Shakespearean tragedy, Hollywood comedy, and English and American Romanticism, play a crucial role in

Cavell's thought, expanding rather than simply illustrating what he takes from philosophers like Wittgenstein, Heidegger, and Austin. In Cavell's work, literature is always bringing to mind philosophy, and philosophy is always opening itself to literature, generating a dialogue that transforms each one.

Cavell's work is literary not only because he quotes literature or even because he respects it. He also treats philosophical texts in literary terms. (I use "literary" and "philosophical" provisionally here, well aware that Cavell's special use of them requires close discussion.) More specifically, he is interested in the stories that traditional epistemologists have told to justify or share their questioning. Cavell brings to life the setting of these stories (Descartes by his fire, Hume in his study), their characters (the solitary thinker and, in Descartes's case, the "malignant demon" who might be deceiving him), and, above all, their examples (Descartes's piece of wax, Hume's table, G. E. Moore's envelope, H. H. Price's tomato). Instead of merely illustrating issues that could be presented in some other way, these stories, in Cavell's view, are necessary to the skeptic's project. In Cavell's reading, the philosophical fate of skepticism is bound up with the stories that the skeptic has to tell.

In addition to exploring the stories of others, Cavell tells numerous tales of his own, parables of doubt, acknowledgment, and avoidance whose novelistic sharpness several readers have praised.[4] He tells these stories, many of them autobiographical, in what Michael Wood has aptly called an "intimate, murmuring style."[5] Mingling argument and autobiography, philosophical and literary references, Continental as well as Anglo-American sources, even using writings from different phases of his own career, Cavell produces in *The Claim of Reason* a kind of intellectual journal or scrapbook that recalls the literary-philosophical-autobiographical hybrids that interest him—*Walden*, for example, and the *Biographia Literaria*.

The reactions of Cavell's readers strengthen the connections that I am broaching here between Cavell's work and some of the Romantic literary texts that have influenced him. When readers dislike Cavell, they echo the complaints that Romantic literature has always generated, finding him self-indulgent, vague, anti-intellectual, and disorganized. Anthony Kenny, for example, calls *The Claim of Reason* a "misshapen, undisciplined amalgam of ill-assorted parts" and Mary Mothersill laments that instead of writing "straight philosophy," Cavell writes a kind of "philosophical criticism" that presumably would not be touched by "the uncovering of fallacious arguments, unsupported premises, or inconsistent principles."[6] Although I am not here assessing Cavell's work, I would argue that my applying Cavell to contemporary criticism partly vindicates his writings. If Cavell's writings were the slipshod performance deplored by some of his critics, I could not have written this book.

More positively, when readers like Cavell, they praise him as others have praised his Romantic models, citing his originality, his honesty, and his ability to connect apparently disparate subjects. Sympathetic readers feel as if they have gotten to know Cavell, even to love him. As Arthur Danto concludes his review of *Pursuits of Happiness:* "This is a voice like no other in philosophy, today or ever, and the only voice it at all resembles is in fiction. . . . In the end I loved the book, loved the author, felt, as with few authors I have read, that I was involved in a relationship something like the one of the couples in the films I still cannot take as seriously as he: as if the experience of reading the book confirms its thought."[7] The couples Danto refers to include Cary Grant and Katharine Hepburn (in *The Philadelphia Story*) and Clark Gable and Claudette Colbert (in *It Happened One Night*) and the relationship that Danto says he enjoys with Cavell's book accordingly resembles a marriage, sustained by the conversation that he and Cavell carry on.

Cavell thus does not simply cite literature, but in his own prose—for better or for worse—draws on the resources of literature in responding to philosophical skepticism, which is why I have said that the neglect of his work by literary theorists is more puzzling than it may first seem. "Neglect" may be too crude a word here. Cavell himself has suggested that while he is not "unaccepted or unknown," he is nevertheless "sub-textual, below the line"—a cited writer but not a systematically studied one (July 2, 1984, letter). Cav-

ell's work is admittedly difficult and depends on philosophical as well as literary sources but much the same could be
said of Derrida, who seems popular by comparison. Many
things account for the reception of Cavell and Derrida by
English and comparative literature departments—fashion,
for example, and American culture's undervaluing its own
achievements (Cavell calls this our Charles Ives or Charles
Sanders Peirce problem). I want to suggest here that the special way in which Cavell's writing is difficult has also contributed to the lack of sustained attention given him.

As is by now well known, the difficulty of Derrida's writing derives in part from its esoteric references, its labyrin-
thine sentences, and, maybe above all for the uninitiated, its
abstruse terminology, its relying on *differance, pharmakon,*
and other exotic terms, many of them multilingual puns that
make sense only when read (some deconstructive commentators on Derrida appropriately call these terms "neograph-
isms," indicating the importance of spelling and appearance
to their meaning—and adding another out-of-the-ordinary
term to the deconstructionist lexicon). De Man's work similarly appears recondite, at least to new readers, because of
its technical rhetorical terms and strenuous cosmopolitan
wordplay, as in this sentence from *The Rhetoric of Romanticism*: "If one gallicizes *antigrav* by hearing the French 'grave'
in 'grav,' then one can hear in *antigrav* a rejection of
the seriousness connoted by *Gesetz der Schwere*, in which
Schwere has all the implications of *Schwermut* and heavy-
heartedness."[8]

Cavell's vocabulary, by contrast, sounds not only much
simpler but also embarrassingly quaint, at least to ears that
have been listening to theorists like de Man. He speaks, for
example, of what is "natural" and "necessary" to human
beings and praises "ordinary" usage as well as everyday,
domestic life. Taken out of context, a statement by Derrida
looks obscure, whereas a statement by Cavell sounds senti-
mental or trite. Cavell's sources, moreover, seem so limited.
In contrast to Derrida, he has taken up only a handful of
already much discussed writers, to whom he repeatedly returns, sometimes deepening his view of them by looking
one more time at a familiar phrase (for instance, "what *we*

do is to bring words back from their metaphysical to their everyday use" in Wittgenstein), sometimes broadening his view by placing them in a new context (juxtaposing Kant to Frank Capra, say, or the comedy of remarriage in Hollywood films to *The Rime of the Ancient Mariner*).[9] To write, for Cavell as well as for Thoreau, is "to give or take readings . . . of whatever is before you" (PAL, 20); that may include books of philosophy and literature but it does not have to. Finally, so many of Cavell's themes, like Wittgenstein's and Wordsworth's, are accordingly arrived at out of school, not just at the movies but even at home with his family, not by reading additional books but by reviewing obvious moments in familiar ones (like the opening scene in *King Lear*). In Cavell, as in Wittgenstein, "we are all teachers and all students—talkers, hearers, overhearers, hearsayers, believers, explainers; we learn and teach incessantly, indiscriminately" (WPC, 40), outside as well as inside universities.

I have remarked elsewhere that a writer like Derrida is not born but made—in the libraries, graduate schools, and professional associations whose assumptions about texts he questions.[10] I am suggesting here that Cavell, while speaking from within academic philosophy, also attends to the many different "forms of life which grow language" (CR, 170) and everything else that interests him, bearing out his sense that "'learning' is not as academic a matter as academics are apt to suppose" (CR, 171). For Cavell, "what there is to be known philosophically remains unknown not through ignorance . . . but through a refusal of knowledge, a denial, or a repression of knowledge" (IQO, 188): "knowledge" here refers to "things that ordinary human beings cannot help thinking about, or anyway cannot help having occur to them" (TS, 9). Cavell's appreciation of nonacademic experience and his devaluation of expertise have helped make him even harder to accommodate than Derrida, who at least offers his readers the hope that they can understand him by mastering his abstruse terminology and sources. Commentators on deconstruction appropriately deal with a number of texts and approaches that the new student must assimilate (Jonathan Culler cites Heidegger, the Frankfurt school, Derrida, Sartre, Foucault, Serres, Lyotard, and Deleuze at the outset of *On Deconstruction*[11]). While the names may be strange and the material complex, the task (making up a reading list) is nevertheless reassuringly familiar to any graduate student, maybe even welcome. A bibliography on Cavell seems disappointingly short and well-worn by comparison (who hasn't already read *Walden* or the "Intimations" Ode?) and a Cavell glossary seems as superfluous as defining "ordinary" and "acknowledgment," to mention only two of his key terms. Appreciating Cavell means not just valuing everyday life and ordinary language but trying to hold onto their considerable insights. For an academic reader Cavell is thus difficult in a disconcerting way, one reason for his lack of influence.

I do not wish to exaggerate Cavell's iconoclasm nor do I want to suggest that I am the first critic to call recent criticism, especially deconstruction, "skeptical." Eugene Goodheart, for example, has entitled his survey of contemporary theory *The Skeptic Disposition in Contemporary Criticism*.[12] By "skeptic" Goodheart means a disposition to question the existence of texts, objective reality, authors, stable meanings, and all the other "god terms" of traditional humanism. In "On Stanley Cavell," Jay Cantor uses the term in a similar way when he calls deconstruction "a thoroughly skeptical enterprise":

> Deconstruction is a version of skepticism which attacks the claim of consciousness that it has at its disposal a language that is representative of the world or even of itself. Signifiers cannot, deconstructive writers argue, be adequately, reliably, aligned with signifieds. . . . Deconstruction is a classical skeptical argument, recast using linguistic metaphors.[13]

Finally, along similar lines, Charles Altieri in *Act and Quality* treats "Derridean arguments as a sophisticated form of skepticism," and in "Construing and Deconstructing," M. H. Abrams parallels several of Derrida's procedures to David Hume's in order to show that "in many of its consequences . . . Derrida's counterphilosophical linguistic ploy converges with those of Hume's skeptical philosophy."[14]

Critics of deconstruction like Goodheart, Abrams, and

Altieri are not the only ones to align it with philosophical skepticism. In *Deconstruction Theory and Practice* Christopher Norris also touches on the resemblance between Derrida and Hume, suggesting that the deconstructionist works at the same "giddy limit" as the skeptic, "suspending all that we take for granted about language, experience and the 'normal' possibilities of human communication." Like Hume's skepticism, Norris concludes, deconstruction is "an activity of thought which cannot be consistently acted on—that way madness lies—but which yet possesses an inescapable rigour of its own."[15]

Many of these same critics who link deconstruction to skepticism—whether to praise Derrida or to fault him—find in Wittgenstein, Austin, or some other version of ordinary-language philosophy a possible antidote to deconstructive doubt. Altieri puts Wittgenstein's importance this way: the *Philosophical Investigations*[16] and other later works offer a means not of satisfying Derrida's demand for absolutely reliable criteria in interpretation but of dispensing with it. In Wittgenstein, as Altieri reads him, there is no natural or divinely ordained center to constrain the free play of meaning, but there need not be one. We arrive at what Altieri frequently calls probabilistic criteria enforced by admittedly contingent forms of life.[17] In *The Deconstructive Turn*, Norris takes a similar tack, but for him Wittgenstein is a cure that will not quite take. For Norris, Wittgenstein's writings, like Austin's, "stand in a distinctly ambivalent relation to those very forms of self-induced sceptical doubt which Wittgenstein professedly chased off limits."[18]

Although indebted to these other accounts, my own characterization of the skeptic and, for that matter, Wittgenstein borrows from Cavell's portrayal of them. I want to emphasize that I am not evaluating Cavell's treatment of skepticism or even explicating it in its entirety. In borrowing from Cavell, I am taking only what I need to address certain issues raised by contemporary literary theory. By "skepticism" I thus mean the procedures of the external-world and other-minds skeptic, as delineated by Cavell, mainly in *The Claim of Reason*. I accordingly do not simply equate skepticism with radical uncertainty but with what Cavell calls the skeptical "recital," the story told by the skeptic for reasons that I will be discussing at length in what follows. There may be other forms of skepticism that do not mesh so well with contemporary theory, just as there are tendencies in contemporary theory that resist being labeled "skeptical" even in my special sense of the term. Nevertheless, the affinities between recent theory and skepticism are deep enough to make Cavell's response to Descartes and Hume pertinent to Derrida and de Man.

RECENT THEORY AND skepticism are of course large terms, embracing multitudes of emphases and tendencies. In my next chapter I begin to cut them down to more manageable size by looking at some of the parallels between recent criticism and external-world skepticism, as analyzed by Cavell.

2

THE TEXT AS OBJECT:
LITERARY THEORY AND
EXTERNAL-WORLD SKEPTICISM

IN DESCRIBING THE STRUCTURE of literary works, the New Critics drew on numerous metaphors, likening the organically unified poem to a verbal icon, plant or body, drama, ballet, musical composition, arch, and many other things. These metaphors were not gratuitous but implied what now seems to many critics an unduly optimistic theory of reading. For deconstructionists in particular, questioning the New Critics' confidence in reading has meant "shaking" the structure of the text, thereby exposing what Derrida calls "that secret place in which it is neither construction nor ruin but lability."[1] Subjected to this pressure, the New Critics' well-wrought urn splinters into fragments that no amount of archeological labor can reassemble.[2]

I want here to argue that this deconstructive probing of texts parallels external-world skepticism, as represented by Cavell. The literary theorist questioning the textual object resembles the traditional epistemologist meditating on the piece of wax, tomato, envelope, or desk that necessarily occupies this form of skepticism. In addition to uncovering what I will be calling the unnaturalness of deconstruction, these parallels help to explain the strengths and weaknesses of some influential attacks against it.

IRONY AS A PRINCIPLE OF STRUCTURE

Despite some reports to the contrary, the death of the New Criticism has been greatly exaggerated. Much recent theory remains not only indebted to the New Criticism but often in dialogue with it, using the New Critics' terms as points of departure.[3] In order to understand what many recent critics are saying, we need to see that they are partly responding to still-powerful New Critical ideas of literary structure.

When the New Critics made paraphrase a heresy, they replaced one set of metaphors for literary structure with another. (I do not mean this as a criticism, as if there were some nonmetaphorical way of describing the organization of a literary work.) According to Cleanth Brooks, for example, a poem is not "merely a bouquet of intrinsically beautiful items" from which a summarizing proposition— the poetical equivalent of an artificial flower—can be extracted intact.[4] Similarly, the "'prose-sense' of the poem is not a rack on which the stuff is hung," just as the form is not a kind of envelope that contains without affecting the contents. Finally, ideas in a poem are not simply "wrapped" in emotion or "decorated" with sensuous imagery.

Instead of resembling a bouquet or a container, a poem for Brooks is more like a plant, its parts unable to survive rearrangement or separation from the whole, the whole similarly dependent on its parts. More positively, a poem is like an arch, that is, a "pattern of resolved stresses," or like a play, with "no waste motion" and "no superfluous parts." All these standard New Critical metaphors—and many others that I will not cite here—acknowledge the positive pressure of context and warn against our confusing the poem with any proposition we might pull from it.

This warning stemmed in part from the fear of mistaking poetry for science, where (again according to Brooks) terms are fixed in advance, not modified by the context in which they occur; where propositions are not only able but expected to stand alone (if they are true, they must be true, anywhere and always); and where complexity, tension, ambiguity, paradox, and irony—all honorific terms in literary criticism—are at best distractions and at worst faults. From the point of view of the New Critics, when we mistakenly think that poetry resembles, or ought to resemble, science, we slight the importance of context, uproot terms and statements from the text that nourishes them, and bring them into what Brooks calls an unreal and destructive competition with science, philosophy, and theology. This competition is unreal because the statement that presumably stands for the poem in fact distorts it; it is destructive—Brooks labels it "vicious" and "crippling"—because "as mere statement," the proposition will either seem "flat and obvious" or patently false. Put in competition with the statements of science or philosophy, a literary statement—"Beauty is truth, truth beauty," for example—will presumably lose.

The New Critics thus emphasized not simply the relevance of context but its enabling power. By context, the New Critics meant the "stuff," to use Brooks's word, surrounding the apparent propositions in the poem: feelings, attitudes, images, metaphors, symbols, and other figures of speech. Against the scientist's insistence on the irrelevance of these embellishments, the New Critics affirmed their power to qualify, refine, test, and finally prove the vision of the poem as a whole. For the New Critics, in other words, a statement in a poem is not simply bent like a stick seen in water but given life, like a cutting from a plant. Or as Robert Penn Warren put it, the poet earns his vision "by submitting it to the fires of irony—to the drama of his structure—in the hope that the fires will refine it."[5] There is, then, a vision validated by the poem as a whole. In New Critical terms, there is motion, but "toward a point of rest"; action, resistance, complexity, and tension culminating in resolution; and a "temporal scheme" unfolding rather than unraveling a tightly knit pattern. Instead of ornamenting or corroding the structure of a poem, irony, in short, strengthens it. The thrust and counterthrust in a poem do not tear it apart but shape it, becoming its means of stability.

Even some of the most influential early critics of the New Criticism—critics as otherwise different as R. S. Crane, E. D. Hirsch, and Northrop Frye—continued to see the poem as (among many other things) an object with a fixed, though intricate, structure. Crane's neo-Aristotelianism led him to picture the poetic work as a "concrete object" or "concrete whole," with a discernible "governing form." (In chapter 7 of the *Poetics*, Aristotle had argued that a well-constructed tragedy, like a "perspicuous" object, must be of a certain magnitude—not too short, like a small and therefore confusing picture, or too long, like a vast object that "the eye cannot take . . . in all at once," but of "a length which can be easily embraced by the memory," like an object that we can see "in one view.") Crane,

of course, objected to the New Critics' deducing the structure of a text from such general a priori qualities as irony,
paradox, and ambiguity. In place of the New Critics' "gen-
eralizing and reductive" method, he offered his own "con-
structive and differentiating" one, which presumably gave
him "a means of isolating and defining those principles of
structure in individual poems which distinguish them from
other poems or kinds of poems and determine thus in
highly specific ways what their distinctive elements are and
the artistic reasons that justify the particular configurations
we observe them to have."[6] Even so, for Crane as well as for
the New Critics, a poem, like "any individual object" (a
man, say, or a couch, to cite only two of his examples), ex-
hibits a distinctive shape and, in the case of literary objects,
arouses a determinate sequence of emotional effects.

Similarly, for E. D. Hirsch, a poem displays an "unchang-
ing and reproducible" structure—reproducible, that is, by
the interpreter. From Hirsch's point of view, the design of a
poem suggests a designer or author: more strongly, one cannot settle on the probable shape of a text—what Hirsch calls
its pattern of emphasis—without appealing to the typical
outlook of the author who made it. Still, for Hirsch, too, a
poem is a bounded, "intentional object," "self-identical"
through different "intentional acts." At one point Hirsch remarks that textual meaning is not a "naked given like a
physical object."[7] But most of his analogies for interpretation are taken from our experience with objects, as in this
largely overlooked passage that I will be returning to:

> When I look at a box, then close my eyes, and then
> reopen them, I can perceive in this second view the
> identical box I saw before. Yet, although I perceive the
> same box, the two acts of seeing are distinctly differ-
> ent—in this case temporally different. The same sort of
> result is obtained when I alter my acts of seeing spa-
> tially. If I go to another side of the room, or stand on a
> chair, what I actually "see" alters with my change in
> perspective, and yet I still "perceive" the identical box;
> I still understand that the *object* of my seeing is the
> same. Furthermore, if I leave the room, and simply re-
> call the box in memory, I still understand that the *object*

I remember is identical with the object I saw. For if
I did not understand that, how could I insist that I
was remembering? The examples are paradigmatic: All
events of consciousness, not simply those involving
visual perception and memory, are characterized by
the mind's ability to make modally and temporally
different *acts* of awareness refer to the same *object* of
awareness. An object for the mind remains the same
even though what is "going on in the mind" is not
the same. The mind's "object" therefore may not be
equated with psychic process as such; the mental object is self-identical over against a plurality of mental
acts.[8]

Hirsch's emphasis on the object in this passage (he italicizes
"object" three times) carries over into his discussion of literary structure. For him, different acts of reading—putting
the book down and picking it up again, five seconds or five
years later (the critical counterpart of closing and then re-
opening our eyes in the box analogy); reviewing in memory
or in fact something we have already read; or looking ahead
to the end—all intend the same textual object.

More generally, for Hirsch, reading a text, like exploring
a box from different vantage points, progresses toward a
determinate image of the text's intended shape. Like many
other students of interpretation before him, including
Crane, Hirsch acknowledges an unavoidable circularity in
reading: as we read, we derive the whole from the parts
while reinterpreting the parts in light of the whole. Nevertheless, for him the give-and-take between part and whole
ends not in an undecidable oscillation among several possible wholes but in a definite pattern inscribed by the historical author.

Finally, Northrop Frye, for all his many disagreements
with the New Critics, has consistently reaffirmed the New
Critics' confidence in the organic unity of the literary work.
In reasserting some familiar New Critical metaphors for literary structure and even applying them to literature as a
whole, Frye has astutely emphasized the sanguine view of
reading that these tropes suggest. According to Frye, although it takes time to experience a literary work, recurring

images, characters, and so on construct a pattern. As the work "moves along in time," it thus also "is spread out in space." Recalling Aristotle's point in chapter 7 of the *Poetics*, Frye observes in the *Anatomy* that

> the word *narrative* or *mythos* conveys the sense of movement caught by the ear, and the word *meaning* or *dianoia* conveys, or at least preserves, the sense of simultaneity caught by the eye. We *listen to* the poem as it moves from beginning to end, but as soon as the whole of it is in our minds at once we "see" what it means. More exactly, this response is not simply to *the* whole *of* it, but to *a* whole *in* it: we have a vision of meaning or *dianoia* whenever any simultaneous apprehension is possible. . . . [A] poem's meaning is literally its pattern or integrity as a verbal structure.[9]

All at once—but really after the hard, purposive work of reading—we see what the work as a whole means.

I will be returning to Frye's identification of meaning with structure. But for now I want to emphasize that Frye in his own way is making much the same point as the other critics I have been discussing. Despite their considerable differences, for all these critics, after some (or much) fiddling, a literary work clicks into focus and its pattern becomes clear. While all these critics allow for disorganization in literature, they all see organic unity as a property of some poems. "See," as Frye observes, is the right word here: literature, on this account, has a spatial as well as a temporal dimension. The text is a highly wrought object as well as an action or story unfolding in time. In the New Critics' terms, the dramatic tension, resistance, and struggle involved in reading a text climax in a point of rest; in Crane's terms, proposing, testing, and revising hypotheses about the overall form of the work terminate in our grasping its shape; in Hirsch, shuttling back and forth between part and whole weaves a fixed and reproducible pattern; and in Frye, *mythos* works not against *dianoia* but for it. From this point of view, then, a literary work, or at least a good literary work, is necessarily a perfect unity, like a well-formed object that we can take in at a glance.

SOLICITING THE STRUCTURE OF A TEXT

Earlier I quoted Derrida on "shaking" a text to spot its points of stress and weakness. "This operation," he goes on to say, "is called (from the Latin) *soliciting*. In other words, *shaking* in a way related to the *whole* (from *sollus*, in archaic Latin 'the whole,' and from *citare*, 'to put in motion')." An unshaken whole, he suggests, is not simply motionless (i.e., not yet put in motion) but dead; killing it, moreover, or making it stand still, is a necessary precondition for seeing it as a whole and thus detecting its structure. As Derrida notes: "The relief and design of structures appears more clearly when . . . [the] living energy of meaning . . . is neutralized. Somewhat like the architecture of an uninhabited or deserted city, reduced to its skeleton by some catastrophe of nature or art," thus no longer bustling with any activity obscuring or changing its shape.[10] (Along similar lines, Paul de Man has noted that "a mythologist like Frye . . . is given license to order and classify the whole of literature into one single thing which, even though circular, would nevertheless be a gigantic cadaver," as if murdering literature—turning it into a "gigantic cadaver"—were necessary to seeing it as a classifiable "single thing.")[11] Shaking the text accordingly means setting it in motion, animating it, or bringing it back to life, allowing its energy to burst or at least to blur the static form previously imposed on it. In light of my preceding section, I should say: previously imposed on it by such otherwise different critics as the New Critics, Crane, Hirsch, and Frye. In "soliciting" the allegedly stable structure of the text, poststructuralist critics are not upending a straw man, as has sometimes been supposed, but reacting to an important tendency in twentieth-century Anglo-American theory. The New Critic W. K. Wimsatt appropriately chose "Battering the Object" as the title of his late essay on some of the developments anticipating deconstruction.[12]

In the work of Derrida and other poststructuralists, this unsettling the text, or "battering the object," can proceed along the following lines. First, these critics often take up a particular interpretive claim. Generally bordering on a critical commonplace, the claim restates the received view of a well-known text, passage, or author. Milton is the author of *Lycidas, Lycidas* is a pastoral, and Jane Austen pokes fun at Mr. Collins in *Pride and Prejudice* are a few such claims mentioned in Stanley Fish's *Is There a Text in This Class?* [13] These statements are attributed to the general reader (Fish cites Wayne Booth's remark that he has never found a reader of *Pride and Prejudice* who does not see any joke played on Mr. Collins), to the academic literary community, or to a well-established, "canonical" critic—a Frye or M. H. Abrams, for example, if the text in question is a Romantic one, a Jean Starobinski if the author is Rousseau.

Secondly, the critic reviewing the claim inquires about its basis, asking, in effect, How do we know that Milton wrote *Lycidas* or that *Lycidas* is a pastoral? Coming from someone outside (or not yet in) the academic critical community— a freshman, say, or a physicist—this question can reflect genuine curiosity about someone else's work. But coming from someone not simply in the academic profession but at its putative summit—at Yale, for instance, or Duke—the question can seem disingenuous, not so much an honest inquiry as a trap that the questioner is setting. (I say this not to dismiss the question, only to pose the problem of its status, to which I will return.)

Third, after requesting the basis of the claim, the critic reproduces the evidence thought to be in its favor. Usually the evidence consists of the text itself (if the critic making the claim is a New Critic), the intention of the author, or some combination of the two (as in Hirsch and Crane). Most importantly, the solidity of this evidence—its right to be called evidence—seems bound up with its priority and independence. To qualify as evidence, it must be there before the interpreter arrives on the scene to discover the facts rather than to manufacture or manipulate them.

Fourth, confronted with this evidence, the poststructuralist critic tries to unsettle or "shake" it, giving it "one final twist," as J. Hillis Miller frequently puts it. In "Force and Signification," Derrida suggests that virtually any statement about a work—"*Lycidas* is a pastoral" will do—implies that the work is simultaneously present to the reader in its en-

tirety. But, Derrida argues, in thinking that we see the complete work, we ignore not only the making of the text but
our reading it. In Derrida's words, we ignore "the history
of the meaning of the work itself" as we wend our way
through it and the history "of its *operation*" on us as we
struggle to grasp it. "The history of the work," Derrida concludes, "is not only its *past*, the eve or the sleep in which it
precedes itself in an author's intentions, but is also the
impossibility of its ever being *present*, of its ever being sum-
marized by some absolute simultaneity or instantaneous-
ness. This is why . . . there is no space of the work, if by
space we mean presence and synopsis."[14] Calling *Lycidas* a
pastoral thus depends upon what Derrida calls "the myth of
a total reading or description"—a myth because we do not
here and now see all of the text.[15] We cannot: it is never
absolutely or simultaneously present to us.

In an important early essay, "Form and Intent in the
American New Criticism," de Man takes a similar tack.
"True understanding," the goal of the interpretative process, always aims at totality, and the idea of totality in turn
"suggests closed forms that strive for ordered and consis-
tent systems and have an almost irresistible tendency to
transform themselves into objective structures" (BI, 31),
such as well-wrought urns and well-grounded arches. Yet,
de Man continues, "the temporal factor, so persistently forgotten, should remind us that the form is never anything
but a process on the way to its completion" (BI, 31)—forever
on the way to completion, de Man adds, because "the act of
understanding is a temporal act that has its own history, but
this history forever eludes totalization. Whenever the circle
seems to close"—whenever the text seems about to congeal
or crystallize into an object—"one has merely ascended or
descended one more step on Mallarmé's '*spirale vertigineuse
conséquente*'" (BI, 32) (to mix several metaphors). For Hirsch,
again, in the analogy described earlier, a box is a box is a
box (just as a text is a text is a text), now as well as five
minutes or five years later: the unseen reduces to the not-
yet-seen and the (temporarily) hidden seems continuous
with what is already in full view.[16] But for de Man, "the
hermeneutic understanding is always, by its very nature,

lagging behind," never catching up with the "mystery" of what stays hidden, the something more ever about to be revealed (BI, 32). A "box" (the quotation marks become obligatory) turns out to be another tunnel in what de Man calls the endless "temporal labyrinth of interpretation" (BI, 35).

In these comments, de Man and Derrida would seem to have the reader coming and going or, more exactly, moving and standing still. When we are stationary, not turning the page or going on to the next line, we cannot see all the work's structure. But when we move, we can never see enough of it. We cannot keep it all in our memory or read so fast as to appear not to be reading. In our necessary but always unsuccessful effort to complete the form, we resemble a base runner trying to circle the bases while holding on to each one. Something has got to give, and for de Man and Derrida it is the myth of a synoptic, finished reading and the text as an object or concrete whole.

In emphasizing these critics' consequent frustration or impatience with reading, I have, of course, overlooked the pleasure that they sometimes associate with it. Deconstructing the text frees these critics to play with it and "not to worry" about getting it right—or so many passages in recent theory would seem to argue. Instead of picturing reading as a source of anxiety, as I am doing, these passages align it with bliss, with what Derrida calls in a famous passage "the Nietzschean *affirmation,* that is the joyous affirmation of the play of the world and of the innocence of becoming, the affirmation of a world of signs without fault, without truth, and without origin which is offered to an active interpretation" but presumably denied to a passive one nostalgically "turned towards the lost or impossible presence of the absent origin." In my view, critics have exaggerated Derrida's hedonism here. He goes on to say that for him there is no question of choosing between these two attitudes toward interpretation. In affirming free play, the Nietzschean affirmation "tries to pass beyond man and humanism," but its dissatisfaction with "man and humanism" makes it impossible as well as appealing. For Derrida, we can no more escape anxiety, desire, insecurity, guilt, nostalgia, and sadness than we can transcend our humanity, "the name of man being the name of that being who, throughout the history of metaphysics or of ontotheology—in other words, throughout his entire history—has dreamed of full presence, the reassuring foundation, the origin and the end of play." We humans can neither renounce this dream nor see it come true. In the terms that I have been using in this chapter, we can neither decipher the structure of a text nor quit worrying about it. We are not gods who can see a text all at once (and thus really see it) or exuberant Nietzschean supermen who can stop trying.[17]

Though taking different routes—one directed toward the reader, or community of readers, and the other directed toward the text—Stanley Fish and J. Hillis Miller reach a conclusion comparable to that of de Man and Derrida. In *Is There a Text in This Class?* Fish takes up what we are tempted to call obviously wrong readings of familiar texts—an Eskimo reading of "A Rose for Emily," for instance, and a gastrointestinal reading of "The Tyger." While these readings seem impossible, Fish wants to say that they are not. The boundaries of texts change—within the course of a reading (as we read, we continuously shape and reshape the text), across interpretive communities (as different groups assign different shapes to texts), and within the lifetime of individuals and cultures (we change the text as we change our mind or, what is the same thing for Fish, as we move in and out of different interpretive communities). Allowing for fluctuation in these instances keeps the possibility of change alive everywhere. Nothing for Fish is finally impossible, not even reading "The Tyger" as an allegory of an unfortunate meal. Fish is not saying that texts lack shape, only that whatever shape we happen to assign them reflects the temporal and local imperatives of our interpretive community.

For Miller, at least in *Fiction and Repetition* and *The Linguistic Moment*, a text oscillates among logically incompatible possibilities, no one of which we can settle on. We can assign a design to the shimmering text only by ignoring the recalcitrant details that jeopardize our choice. And altering an interpretive guess in one place only causes trouble in another. Instead of stopping this play of meaning, going outside the text only prolongs it. For example, bringing in the author, as Hirsch would advise, in search of something prior to the text or free of its ambiguity means bringing in more (undecidable) texts—diaries, letters, and other works that defer the definitive reading that we want from them. For Miller, then, although we cannot do without reading, we cannot do with it what we supposedly want, namely, find in the text a "structural principle which will allow [us] to find its secret, explicate it once and for all, untie all its knots and straighten all its threads."[18] Put differently, the "un-involved spectator"—the reader who refuses to enter the text—"sees nothing but a confused spectacle, and so sees nothing." But the "involved actor"—the reader who tries to work through the text—"is always a victim of [its] per-petually renewed power of disremembering, and so he too sees nothing but a confused spectacle." Reading is thus for Miller, as for de Man and Derrida, an interminably "frus-trating activity," "a remembering that is at the same time a forgetting," which "never succeeds in holding the whole text in an absolute clarity of understanding all in the mind at once."[19]

For all these critics, we accordingly cannot call *Lycidas* a pastoral—we cannot call *Lycidas* "Lycidas"—without either stifling the endlessly vibrating text or trying to escape the inescapable temporal predicament of reading. The fifth (and final) step in this argument brings out what has been at stake: if we cannot call *Lycidas* a pastoral, then what can we claim to say about it? Loosely put, the answer would seem to be nothing, or not as much as we thought. This does not mean that we quit or even ought to quit talking, as Hirsch and others have supposed. (At the outset of "Objective In-terpretation," Hirsch says, "If textual meaning itself could change, contemporary readers would lack a basis for agree-ment or disagreement. No one would bother seriously to discuss such a protean object," a "protean object" for Hirsch being something close to a contradiction in terms.[20]) But while talk about the text continues, its objectivity or finality is now forever suspect. Put differently, instead of vanishing, the text reappears as a spur-of-the-moment construct or ad hoc fabrication, shorn of its evidentiary status, its independence, priority, and fixity—everything, in short, that made such otherwise different critics as the New Critics, Hirsch, Crane, and Frye want to liken the text to a closed form or well-wrought object.

The preceding account, of course, traces only one path among many taken by such complex writers as Derrida, Fish, and de Man. I want here to suggest some parallels between this line of thought and tendencies in external-world skepticism, as characterized by Cavell. One way to bring out these parallels would be to show that the same poststructuralist arguments used to unsettle texts also apply to objects—that objects, from this point of view, are as elusive, or protean, as the texts that the New Critics saw as organic wholes. In this section I will be taking a slightly different approach, one that moves from traditional external-world skepticism back to the argument in literary theory that I have just described. A casual remark by Fish in *Is There a Text in This Class?* anticipates what I will be doing. To illustrate the point that we explain unfamiliar material by drawing on what our audience already knows, Fish cites the example of a philosopher to whom we might introduce recent literary theory by referring to "that philosophical tradition in which the stability of objects has always been a matter of dispute."[21] I want now to offer one view of that tradition, taken from Cavell's *Claim of Reason*.

I turn to external-world skepticism not so much to explain it as to shed light on some important moments in the literary theorist's "battering" the textual object, in particular the choice of a well-known text or passage and the strain that results when the theorist tries to make us question what we can know, or say, about the example. Finally, by drawing on external-world skepticism, I want to show why some attacks on recent theory are at once justified and unsuccessful.

According to Cavell, the external-world skeptic performs a "skeptical recital" that in skeletal form looks like this:

1. CLAIM: Consider this piece of wax (or any other generic object, a term I will be defining).

2. REQUEST FOR BASIS: How do you (or I) know it is there?
3. BASIS: Because I see it (or feel it or in some way sense it).
4. GROUND FOR DOUBT: But do you see all of it?
5. MORAL: No. I therefore don't really know that the piece of wax is actually there. This conclusion has the force of asserting I can't really claim to know that anything is actually there, anything that I "know" by means of my senses.

Cavell culls this recital from the writings of such diverse traditional epistemologists as Descartes and Hume. While the details may vary, the format remains basically the same.

In step 1, the philosopher focuses on a familiar object in part to set the stakes as high as possible. If knowledge fails here, where the task is apparently only to recognize a common object under optimal conditions, then knowledge fails everywhere and always—or so the skeptic insists. In order to justify a general conclusion about knowledge, the philosopher thus constructs a best case—using a generic object in full view, readily seen by anyone.

By a generic object, Cavell means an object that in a particular context solicits recognition rather than identification—a desk rather than an escritoire, a bird rather than a goldfinch. I take this last example from J. L. Austin's "Other Minds," which offers the following version of the skeptical recital:

CLAIM: There is a goldfinch in the garden.
REQUEST FOR BASIS: How do you know?
BASIS: From the red head.
GROUND FOR DOUBT: But that's not enough; woodpeckers also have red heads.

After citing this dialogue, Cavell goes on to quote Austin's conclusion:

I don't by any means *always* know whether it's one or not. It may fly away before I have a chance of testing it, or of inspecting it thoroughly enough. This is simple enough: yet some are prone to argue that because I *sometimes* don't know or can't discover, I *never* can. (Quoted in CR, 133)

In Cavell's view, Austin has characteristically stacked the deck against skepticism.[22] For one thing, a goldfinch does not count as a generic object here: failing to identify a goldfinch in this case (or to make sure that it is not a woodpecker) might imply lack of training, hastiness in judgment, or a poor view of the bird. But such a mistake is simple enough, as Austin is quick to point out; it does not threaten knowledge as a whole. The skeptic, again, takes a best case for knowing, where "best" signals the apparent irrelevance of the "contextual matters of opportunity and conditions" that figure in Austin's scenario. As Cavell puts it, "all you have to know, to achieve knowledge in the philosopher's case, is, one could say, how to talk" (CR, 134). (Cavell's claim here would seem to be confirmed by picture books that teach children how to talk or at least how to recognize certain letters by displaying generic objects, with an apple standing for *A*, a ball for *B*, and so on.) In addition, Austin's suggestion that the skeptic is only "prone to argue" his case misconstrues what the skeptic regards as the argument's inevitability and makes it seem as if skepticism were merely an (academic?) exercise or idle choice.

Only a best case of knowledge accounts for the precipitousness of external-world skepticism. Knowledge of the world depends on knowledge of this object—this desk, this piece of wax, that anyone can recognize. When this object goes or suddenly seems questionable, the world goes—instantly, irreversibly. The argument in literary theory that I traced earlier strives for a similar effect by focusing on a canonical or widely read text or author familiar to anyone who speaks the language of literary criticism—a Shelley as opposed to a Crabbe (in *Deconstruction and Criticism*) or "The Tyger" instead of *An Island in the Moon* (in *Is There a Text in This Class?*). Critics of recent theory often cite its adherence to canonical texts and authors as more or less surprising evidence of its conservatism, contrasting deconstructionists in particular to activist critics more obviously committed to opening the canon and writing about texts that arbitrary criteria have kept marginal. While I agree with this charge (in fact, I have offered a version of it in *Does Deconstruction Make Any Difference?*) I would add that the deconstructionist's choice of texts reflects not only a political predisposition but the demands of an argument that seeks to generate doubt about the very possibility of reading. Virtually everyone concedes that some assertions about literary works rest on shakier grounds than others—that Ernest Jones's reading of Hamlet's alleged procrastination, say, is more problematic than his calling the play a tragedy. The deconstructionist wishes to show that doubts infect even "best cases," that is, claims about texts that seem to require little specialized knowledge and ideological persuasion. I say "seem to" because the deconstructionist's point, of course, is that even these apparently obvious or factual claims are at bottom questionable. A comment by Stanley Corngold captures the severe disorientation that results: "Whatever the motive, the deconstruction of a difference is never allowed to remain a local instance. De Man reads all local instances of indetermination only to point to a universal void of indetermination."[23]

In using the external-world skeptic's generic object to account for the literary theorist's canonical example, or local instance of indetermination, I do not mean to identify the literary and the philosophical arguments. Compared with a desk, "The Tyger" is obviously complicated and even esoteric. But compared with *Tiriel*, "The Tyger" is more often anthologized and is therefore more familiar to literary critics, and its meaning, though admittedly complex, thought to be understood. Even so, the fact that knowledge of literature may have to depend on such a refined example limits the impact of the literary theorist's argument. Knowledge of literature does not collapse with knowledge of "The Tyger" in the same abrupt and terrifying way that knowledge of the world goes with knowledge of a desk. More speculation and educated guesswork—and consequently more room for doubt—are involved in reading "The Tyger" than in recognizing a desk. Deconstructing the poem accordingly lacks the jarring effect of questioning the existence of a desk, the "object" taken up by literary criticism being so much more elusive and vulnerable to questioning. In relating deconstruction to external-world skepticism, I am thus not trying to turn "The Tyger" into a desk but to show why "The Tyger" (and not some lesser-known text) is being questioned.

In listening to the external-world skeptic's recital, Cavell tries to determine when the skeptic sounds "unnatural" or out of tune with what is ordinarily said. For Cavell, signs of strain first appear in the skeptic's attempt to supply a reason for doubt by asking "do you see all of it?" or "how much do you really see?" (step 4), where "it" refers to the generic object chosen as an example. While these can be legitimate questions in some contexts, they ordinarily arise when the object in question is not in the full view of the person asking them. They accordingly sound odd in the optimal context constructed by the philosopher. At the very least, their point needs clarifying, as the philosopher implicitly concedes when he adds something like "you don't see the back" or "you don't see the inside," thus trying to coax the understandably confused observer into conceding that the object is in some sense not fully visible. For Cavell, this continuation reduces the peculiarity of the skeptic's question without, however, making it completely natural, because the generic object under investigation—a piece of wax, for instance—lacks clear division into parts such as a back and a front, or an inside and an outside. Or, rather, the object acquires these parts only because when we look at it, we cannot see what we can call at this moment (and this moment only) its back. As Cavell concludes:

> Thus this skeptical picture is one in which all our objects are moons. In which the earth is our moon. In which, at any rate, our position with respect to significant objects is *rooted*, the great circles which establish their back and front halves fixed in relation to it, fixed in our concentration as we gaze at them. The moment we move, the "parts" disappear, or else we *see* what had before been hidden from view. . . . This suggests that what the philosophers call "the senses" are themselves conceived in terms of this idea of a geometrically fixed position, disconnected from the fact of their possession and use by a creature who must *act*. (CR, 202)

When we move, blink, or even breathe, the object returns in full view, or at least we no longer feel that "parts" of it are forever hidden.

Cavell's point should be distinguished from Hirsch's in the box analogy noted earlier. For Hirsch, our past experience with objects obviates our need to inspect one from every angle before deciding that it is probably a box (or, for that matter, before deciding that it is an object). From this point of view, although all of the box is not simultaneously present to us, it does not have to be for us to recognize it. Confronted with an example like Hirsch's, the skeptic asks, among other things, "How do you know that the object you now see (when you reopen your eyes, for instance) is still the same object you saw—the object you claim to remember?" Hirsch does not have much of an answer; he only says, "If it is not the same box, then how can I insist that I am remembering it?" to which the skeptic replies, "Good question. How *can* you insist that you're remembering it?" Rather than try to answer the skeptic's question ("But do you see all of it?"), Cavell initially focuses on the person asking it—the solitary, motionless philosopher staring at an object.

Gazing at an object seems incompatible with what I said earlier about "shaking" or "soliciting" one, but this problem is Derrida's, not Cavell's. Despite his interest in setting the textual object in motion, when Derrida is wondering whether the text is absolutely present to us, he is stationary, trying (and necessarily failing) to penetrate the text or see all of it at once. By contrast, at some point that cannot be specified in advance, Hirsch's reader stops moving (or reading) because he can be fairly sure that the text, say, is a pastoral. Reading comes to an end in a verifiable statement about the text's probable design. Once this statement has been secured, reading further to validate it seems as unnecessary as checking that a box is (still) a box by obsessively exploring it. According to Hirsch, we read further to add to our knowledge, not to confirm or revise it, though this may of course happen. There is room for the unexpected in Hirsch, but not for terminal uncertainty. (My comments on Hirsch here also apply to Frye, who has said that he has a hard time finishing a novel once its archetypal structure has become clear. For Frye, reading further is like fine-tuning an already focused picture.) At some point, Derrida's reader also sits still, not, however, because reading has done its work (of revealing the text's structure) but because the reader can never read fast or intensely enough to see all the text at once, a precondition for really seeing it.

In focusing on the skeptic's questions (steps 2 to 4 in the skeptical recital), Cavell is showing that the skeptic faces the following dilemma. The skeptic cannot divide the object into parts—carving it with an X, say, to mark its front or back—without lessening its generic status and thus its implications for knowledge as a whole. A piece of wax marked with an X is now a particular object shaped in a specific way.[24] If the philosopher thus cannot designate the different parts of the object, neither can he use it as it is. He cannot raise questions about the generic object in this context, or, rather, he can raise them, Cavell says, only "by distorting our life among objects . . . or by constructing an idea of the 'senses' which extirpate[s] them from the body" (CR, 203)[25]—in this case, by (only) staring at the object and not touching or using it.

The literary theorists that I have been discussing get into a similar bind, as Fish's "A Rose for Emily" example suggests. Fish realizes the apparent facetiousness of the question, "How do you know that 'A Rose for Emily' does not describe an Eskimo in the concluding tableau of Emily and her father in the doorway?"—the question that Fish nevertheless must ask at this point in his argument. To mitigate the oddity of this question, he goes on to mention some circumstances that would make it appropriate, "the discovery of a letter in which Faulkner confides that he has always believed himself to be an Eskimo changeling" being one of them.[26] But instead of clarifying his original example, such a letter, like the skeptic's marking the generic object, significantly changes it. Without the letter, the question "How do you know?" idles, or seems motivated only by whim (among many other possibilities). But with the letter Fish's anecdote fails to generate doubt about the possibility of literary knowledge. Instead of challenging the rules of the game, he is now conforming to them, furnishing evidence rather than questioning whether there is such a thing. In the absence of the letter (or something like it), Fish's questioning, in short, languishes; it seems merely the product of someone not yet in the academic interpretive community, a product, in other words, of corrigible ignorance. Adding the letter keeps Fish's recital going, though in a direction that he does not want—toward a new view of Faulkner's story, not toward suspicion of all views.[27]

In Cavell, the opening statement of the skeptic's recital— the claim that "X exists" or "I see X"—turns out to be as problematic as the questions it inspires. According to Cavell, we make an assertion in at least two ways: by telling someone something and by remarking upon something. Not just anything at any time can be told or remarked upon. Telling presupposes a listener who is able not only to understand the utterance but to be informed by it; remarking requires something worth remarking. Like all grammatical stipulations, these imply complex judgments, not a closed set of putatively remarkable or newsworthy topics, like spectacular sunsets or world events. One person's news can be another person's trivia. And while anything can be made the subject of a remark, nothing has to be (a remark, like a joke, can fall flat). Still, to qualify as telling or remarking upon something, a comment must satisfy certain prerequisites, informing someone in the one case and highlighting something worth noticing in the other.

Cavell is working toward the conclusion that no concrete claim is ever entered (i.e., asserted) in the skeptical recital. The philosopher's typical opening move—for example, "I see a tomato"—does not count as telling someone something because the statement in this context does not inform anyone of anything. "I see a tomato" could have the force of an assertion if, say, I were pointing to the tomato I had just found under the table, the tomato we had all been looking for after it rolled off the kitchen counter. Similarly, "I see a tomato" could underscore something unusual, for example, a tomato still growing in the family garden despite yesterday's fire. But in each case the statement becomes a concrete claim only by compromising the best case that the skeptic needs to question knowledge as a whole. Without a concrete claim, then, the skeptical recital cannot get started (the skeptic has nothing to challenge); but with a concrete claim the recital can terminate only in caution or practical advice (like "Look under the table when you drop something in the kitchen"), not in wholesale skeptical doubt.

Fish's *Is There a Text in This Class?* shows that the skeptical

literary theorist again faces an analogous problem. Many of
Fish's examples, as already mentioned, turn on seemingly
axiomatic statements, such as "Milton is the author of *Lycidas*" or "*Lycidas* is a pastoral." I can imagine many times
when critics might say such things, when, that is, these
claims might count as remarks or assertions—for example,
when introducing Milton to a high school class or defining
a pastoral. But these contexts differ from the best case that
Fish has to build. In these contexts, asking "How do you
know?" reflects the momentary uncertainty of a student trying to master something new (Milton or the definition of
"pastoral"). Answering the question accordingly lessens the
student's confusion, maybe even ends it, as in the following
exchange:

> TEACHER: Lycidas is a pastoral.
> STUDENT: How do you know?
> TEACHER: Because Milton borrows the imagery of a
> shepherd's life to lament the death of a friend.

Even if this answer does not easily or instantly satisfy the
questioner, additional questions (in this context) will suggest eventually remedial ignorance instead of leading to in-
corrigible skeptical doubt. At stake is not the possibility of
saying anything valid about *Lycidas* (and thus any literary
work), but the character of the individuals involved—the
student's aptitude, for example, and the teacher's patience
and skill.

CRITICIZING DECONSTRUCTION

In Cavell's commentary on external-world skepticism, what
he calls the skeptic's humanity keeps impeding the progress
of the skeptical recital. The question "But do you see all
of it?" depends on the skeptic's staying perfectly still, barely
breathing, as if in a trance: "It is not just careful description, or practical investigation, under way here. The philosopher is as it were looking for a *response* from the
object, perhaps a shining" (DK, 8). (This picture fits in well
with the deconstructionists' account of their own procedures as close, or slow, reading.) Moving or even blink-

ing breaks the skeptic's intense concentration, frustrating
the motionless, otherworldly position that the skeptic must
maintain if the generic object is to have hidden "parts."
Similarly, instead of solving the skeptic's problem at this
point (step 4), marking the object only reintroduces the
practical activities that must be kept at bay for the recital to
reach a suitably skeptical conclusion. Finally, when we think
about when we might make such a statement as the recital's
opening claim, the resulting scenario fails to threaten
knowledge as a whole. The skeptic feels compelled to assert
that we do not really know that objects exist, though admittedly we act as if they were really there. The fact that as
moving, breathing, social creatures we balk at this conclusion shows that it is unnatural.

"Unnatural," however, does not mean impossible. As
Cavell frequently puts it, nothing could be more human
than the skeptic's dissatisfaction with our ordinary ways of
knowing. Cavell initially credits the skeptic with wishing for
a firmer or more rigorous connection with objects than everyday life seems to allow but he adds, "Deprived of the
ordinary forms of life in which that connection is, and is
alone secured, he [the skeptic] is trying to reestablish it in
his immediate consciousness, then and there" (CR, 238).
The skeptic murders ostensibly to connect (IQO, 198); the
object disappears with his apparent longing it to make it
present.

The skeptic's violence here may be typically male, or so
Cavell has speculated in his most recent writing; hence my
reference to the skeptic as "he" throughout this chapter. It
is as if the sheer existence of the object, its separateness,
creates a gap that the skeptic thinks knowing will bridge or
even obliterate. In Cavell's words, "It is against the (fanta-
sied) possibility of overcoming this hyperbolic separateness
that the skeptic's (disappointed, intellectualized, impossible, imperative, hyperbolic) demand makes sense" (DK,
9)—his demand, that is, to possess or dominate the object,
to establish "an absolute or inalienable bonding to himself"
(DK, 9). Lest it seem as if Cavell were self-indulgently piling
up words here—a charge made by some of his critics—I
should point out that the skeptic's demand is intellectual-

ized in that he would know the object; hyperbolic in that he would really know it, not just "know" it as we ordinarily do; disappointed and finally impossible in that his quest for certainty ends in doubt.

Cavell wonders whether this demand may be masculine or at least "inflected by gender difference" partly, I think, because it generally surfaces in men and partly because it is often expressed as a desire to penetrate the object, as when Derrida describes "soliciting" the text as a "displacement [that] disjoints all the articulations and penetrates all the points welded together by the imitated [i.e., interpreted] discourse."[28] But instead of concluding that skepticism, or "the passion for knowledge as such," arises only in men, Cavell suggests that it may assume a different form in women: "what masculine philosophy knows as skepticism feminine philosophy will know as fanaticism" (DK, 17), as the "fanaticism of unconditioned or hyperbolic love" (DK, 18), a fantasy not of knowing but of being absolutely known.

An influential critique of skepticism, sometimes associated with Austin and more generally with ordinary-language philosophy, focuses on this passion for knowledge, this (possibly male) fantasy of wanting really to know, or penetrate, an object. According to this critique, the skeptic's longing for knowledge goes too far, becoming an obsession with absolute certainty that necessarily ends in doubt—necessarily, because in everyday life we can never be completely sure of anything. But even though we cannot be absolutely certain, we can be sure enough that a particular bird is a goldfinch and not a woodpecker (to use an example from Austin mentioned earlier).

In recent literary theory, deconstruction has been criticized along similar lines by Charles Altieri, M. H. Abrams, and others influenced by ordinary-language philosophy. (Abrams appropriately entitles one of his most important essays on contemporary criticism "How to Do Things with Texts," an obvious allusion to Austin.) According to this familiar reading, Derrida and other recent critics long for certainty in interpretation and inevitably fail to find it—inevitably, because the interpretation of literary texts necessarily appeals to criteria that are flexible, diverse, open-ended, loose, and largely uncodified, especially when contrasted to the firmer criteria of science and logic. Moreover, when we construe the meaning of a text, such seemingly subjective qualities as tact, imagination, and temperament do come into play. But interpretation is not therefore arbitrary, or terminally undecidable, as Derrida would have it. Although we cannot be absolutely sure about the meaning of a text, we can be sure enough to go on as critics, teachers, and readers. From this point of view, deconstructionists inexplicably expect too much. Their commitment to certainty is admirable but out of place in literary criticism and everyday life, where we have to be—more strongly, where we can be—content with probabilities, inferences, educated guesses, and some degree of indeterminacy.

This critique matters because it picks up on what I would call, following Cavell, the unnaturalness of deconstruction. The deconstructionist's doubts about the possibility of literary knowledge do not ordinarily arise—as the deconstructionist is the first to admit—but befall a frustrated, disappointed theorist apparently straining to make a text absolutely and simultaneously present—and failing. But this critique has difficulty explaining why Derrida is such an absolutist blindly in quest of certainty and why, by expecting too much, he brings disappointment on himself. Unable to say what motivates Derrida, Abrams in particular has a hard time appreciating deconstruction, despite the generosity he wants to show it. Conceding that "some of [Derrida's] characteristic modes of verbal and rhetorical play are very infectious," Abrams compares deconstructive criticism to epideictic rhetoric, or "display oratory," in which the critic, instead of trying "to tell us anything we don't know already about his ostensible subject," (merely?) attempts "to display his own invention, verbal and rhetorical skills, and aplomb for the admiration and delight of his audience."[29] At best, deconstruction is entertaining, at worst gratuitous and even dangerous.

This dismissal of deconstruction undercuts the good will

Abrams shows Derrida, de Man, and the other critics he is discussing. What starts out as a fair, painstaking analysis of deconstruction ends up sounding (at least to deconstructionists) like an uncomprehending attack. Faced with a similarly limited critique of skepticism in Austin, Cavell objects that "Austin has no account of [the] emptiness" into which skepticism drifts (TS, 37). Cavell wants to know why the skeptic sets the sights of knowledge too high—why he is drawn "to just *this* form of self-defeat" (IQO, 216–17), why, in other words, he turns an everyday difficulty (e.g., making sure X is a woodpecker) into an epistemological impossibility:

> To suppose [as the ordinary-language philosopher supposes] that the philosopher has done the foolishly self-defeating thing of raising standards (here, standards of certainty) so high that *of course* no human knowledge can attain them, is to treat him as though he had set his heart, say, on having human beings rise ten feet in the air without external prompting, or defined "getting into the air" as "getting ten feet into the air," and then, finding the world high jump record to reach short of eight feet, realized with a shock that no human being can really even get off the ground, and said as consolation to all jumpers, "You jump high enough for practical purposes." (CR, 221–22)

According to Cavell, the quest for certainty itself needs explaining, lest it seem gratuitous or perverse, something the skeptic is only "prone to argue" and everyone else entitled, even encouraged, to forget—again, a conclusion that Abrams reaches, however unwillingly, in his critique of deconstruction.

Explaining the skeptic's motivation takes Cavell from external-world to other-minds skepticism, which entails a move from philosophy to literature, because as Cavell frequently notes, other-minds skepticism remains largely undiscovered by philosophy. In literature, "skepticism's 'doubt' is motivated not by (not even where it is expressed as) a (misguided) intellectual scrupulousness but by a (displaced) denial, by a self-consuming disappointment that seeks world-consuming revenge" (DK, 6). I will be spending much of my next two chapters unraveling this complex statement, which in my view is crucial to Cavell's account of skepticism. I begin in chapter 3 by showing how something resembling other-minds skepticism arises in recent literary theory.

3

READING THE HUMAN FIGURE:
LITERARY THEORY AND
OTHER-MINDS SKEPTICISM

EVEN (OR MAYBE ESPECIALLY) those critics who liken literary texts to well-wrought objects hasten to emphasize the distinctiveness of literary works. Whereas objects, considered as objects, are essentially fixed and dead, literary works, in this view, are vital and infused with such human qualities as spirit, intent, and growth. I am paraphrasing Coleridge, whose influential comments on literary form define literary works as the "results and symbols of living power as contrasted with lifeless mechanism." Coleridge went on to assert optimistically that "no work of true genius dare want its appropriate form, neither indeed is there any danger of this" because the "spirit of poetry, like all other living powers, must of necessity circumscribe itself by rules, were it only to unite power with beauty. It must embody in order to reveal itself; but a living body is of necessity an organized one." A poem, in short, is not so much an object (if by object we mean a manufactured, inert thing) as it is a living body, its "exterior" inevitably functioning as "the physiognomy of the being within."[1]

Coleridge's remarks have licensed numerous analogies between reading poems and people. According to Jacques Barzun, for example, "one reads a poem as one reads a face—with a great deal of attention, knowledge, and experience of reading. There is only this difference, that one may stare at a poem."[2] Wayne Booth similarly observes that "in this respect [i.e., in being themselves and not "*instances* of anything"] the novels, symphonies, paintings, and constitutions that we study are precisely like people themselves: They are not exhaustible by any description or definition, any act of valuation or denigration."[3] And, finally, A. C. Bradley has said that when reading a poem, we no more separate form and meaning than when seeing someone smile, we distinguish "those lines in the face which express a feeling" from "the feeling that the lines express."[4]

I mention these analogies partly because in recent theory they have come under attack as much for what they suggest about people as for what they say about poems. In this chapter, I want to show how these attacks borrow from the imagery and procedures of other-minds skepticism, as characterized by Cavell. "Borrow from" here indicates spiritual affinity more than intellectual indebtedness. In Coleridge and the criticism he has inspired, the text benefits from the intelligibility of the mind, that is, the mind's capacity to express itself, thereby making itself known, in words, gestures, and literary works, among other things. In Derrida and the criticism that he has influenced, the text partakes of the inexpressiveness (sometimes even the nonexistence) of the mind—the mind's inability to control the signs that it nevertheless tries to use.

I begin this chapter by showing how two influential precursors of recent theory—Murray Krieger and Georges Poulet—in different ways see poems as unique objects more akin to especially responsive people than to lifeless things. I then show how Miller, de Man, and Derrida contest the intelligibility and distinctiveness—what Krieger might call the life—of texts. I conclude by once again linking these deconstructive arguments to skepticism, this time to other-minds skepticism, as portrayed by Cavell.

THE TEXT AS BODY: MURRAY KRIEGER AND GEORGES POULET ON LITERARY FORM

In order to show where recent theorists are headed, I again want to sketch some of the New Critical ideas that provoke their theorizing. One good source of these ideas is "Mediation, Language, and Vision in the Reading of Literature," an important essay by Murray Krieger, one of the best and most sympathetic commentators on the New Criticism. Published in 1969, the essay was first read as a paper at a symposium at Johns Hopkins, where Continental challenges to the New Criticism were beginning to affect the work of J. Hillis Miller and other American critics. While acknowledging some shortcomings in the New Criticism, Krieger defends its commitment to contextualism and mediation against the accusations of Ihab Hassan, Georges Poulet, and others. Some of these complaints against the New Criticism foreshadow the rhetoric, though not the intent, of later attacks by de Man and Derrida. Krieger's wide-ranging essay thus provides an especially sophisticated restatement of some New Critical assumptions as well as a glimpse at the developments that would subsequently try to undermine them.

Krieger is trying here to save mediation not only from such "anti-mediators" as Poulet, Hassan, and the early Geoffrey Hartman and Harold Bloom but also from such "over-mediators" as Northrop Frye, Claude Lévi-Strauss, and René Girard. According to Krieger, the anti-mediator, impatient with mere words, wishes to dissolve or circumvent the formal properties of literary texts in order to reach the raw experience that words presumably veil—the mental experience or unmediated self-consciousness of the author, in the case of Poulet, and what Krieger calls "the bodily realities of our instincts," in the case of Hassan. Whereas the anti-mediator tries to replace form with uninhibited subjectivity and particularity, the over-mediator subsumes literary form under broader categories—more general linguistic structures in Lévi-Strauss, archetypes derived from literature as a whole in Frye. For Krieger, much as for Coleridge before him, rescuing the individual literary work from these extremes means proclaiming it "a special object," that is, "one without the object's deadly thereness, its spatial 'fix,' " yet having the object's integrity in that the literary work is there as a public entity for the critic to analyze. At stake here, among many other things, is the status of criticism as "an educating process." Lacking a determinate object, the anti-mediator can produce only "poems about poems" that "impress the imagination more than the understanding," dazzling students but not finally teaching them how to read poetry.[5]

Poulet's "Criticism and the Experience of Interiority," his contribution to the seminal 1966 Johns Hopkins symposium on "The Languages of Criticism and the Sciences of Man," exemplifies what I think Krieger means by "anti-mediation" here. Poulet begins by saying that while books obviously are physical objects, they "are not just objects among others" because they "appear to be lit up" with the hope that someone will "suddenly transform their existence" by reading them. Other objects—Poulet mentions a sewing machine, a plate, and a table—do not suggest an interior dimension that we wish to explore. These objects only ask, if they ask anything, "to be alone." They can "dispense with any interference from the mind." A book, by contrast, forever offers itself to a reader: "It asks nothing better than to exist outside itself, or to let you exist in it. In short, the extraordinary fact in the case of a book is the falling away of the barriers between you and it. You are inside it; it is inside you; there is no longer either outside or inside."[6]

According to Poulet, when we read, thereby accepting the book's constant invitation to open it, we realize that we are no longer simply holding an object but becoming aware of a consciousness, "the consciousness of another, no different from the one I automatically assume in every human being I encounter, except that in this case the consciousness is open to me, welcomes me, lets me look deep inside itself, and even allows me, with unheard-of license, to think what it thinks and feel what it feels" (p. 57). In reading, then, the "object wholly object," or, as Coleridge would have it, the object *as* object, "is no more" (p. 57). Its disappearance underscores the pliability of literary objects, their characteristic yielding "with little resistance to the importunities of the mind," as well as their compatibility with our own consciousness. When we read, Poulet says, we think the thoughts of another as if they were our own.

This other, Poulet continues, is not simply the author, although because "every word of literature is impregnated with the mind of the one who wrote it," Poulet does allow for an "analogy" between a writer's works and life (p. 61). Even so, the subject whose thoughts we think while reading lives only in the work itself. Nothing external to the work shares or needs to reinforce its hold on us. The self-sufficiency of the work means "that so long as it is animated by this vital inbreathing inspired by the act of reading, a work of literature becomes at the expense of the reader whose own life it suspends a sort of human being, that is a mind conscious of itself and constituting itself in me as the subject of its own objects" (p. 62). The work, in other words, needs the reader to inspirit it or at least to allow it to live. But once alive it does not need an author to sustain it. The work has become a kind of human being, more accessible than other people in other contexts and more dependent on our animating it, but still a person living its own life in us.

Poulet goes on to chart various ways of relating to the special interior or subjectified (i.e., literary) object. Each tells a story predicated on the analogy between a literary text and a person that I have just mentioned. Jean Starobinski, for example, seems to Poulet an optimistic, even utopian, reader, who is like Rousseau in his "yearning for an immediate transparence of all beings to each other, which would enable them to understand each other in an ecstatic happiness," as in the *fête citadine* or *fête champêtre* (p. 67). Starobinski's criticism accordingly strives for "perfect agreement" not simply between the mind of the author and the mind of the reader but between the text and reader as "incarnate beings," "the particularities of [whose] physical existence constitute not obstacles to understanding, but rather a complex of supplementary signs, a veritable language which must be deciphered and which enhances mutual comprehension" (p. 68). But after achieving intimacy with the textual object, Starobinski retreats, at once "avoiding the encumbrances of too prolonged a life in common" (p. 68) and establishing a perspective from which he can assess the object from afar. His criticism thus concludes with a farewell "exchanged between two beings who have begun by living together," the one left behind (presumably the text) continuing to be illuminated by the one that moves on (the reader).

Poulet faults Starobinski not for penetrating the object but for penetrating it too easily, for passing through its form without respecting its intractability. In Starobinski, "literary works lose their opacity, their solidity, their objective dimension, like those palace walls which become transparent in certain fairy tales" (p. 69). Poulet wishes neither to minimize the objective elements of a work (Starobinski's error) nor to rivet on them (the mistake of formalism) but to move through them to an intentional consciousness that inheres in the text but transcends it and stands alone. When seeing a collection of works by Tintoretto, for example, Poulet suddenly senses a common essence, which can be grasped only when he empties his mind of the particular paintings that suggest it. For Starobinski, as Poulet describes him, form is adequate to the consciousness it expresses; hence his untroubled, effortless transition from the object to the subjectivity disclosed in it. For Poulet, however, there is always a residue of subjectivity, implied but never finally contained by the objective form of the text, a something that forever surpasses outward show (to paraphrase Hamlet). Uncovering this remnant of consciousness in all its ineffability, "fundamental indeterminacy," and transcendence requires not simply seeing the form or even seeing through it but annihilating it, the only way to apprehend this "subjectivity without objectivity" (p. 72). When asked how he would criticize a mistaken identification of the admittedly ineffable essence of Tintoretto (by a bad student, say), Poulet accordingly replies, "I would try to identify with my bad student, and I would not be able to do it; I would fail in this effort of identification. The sole criterion that I would have that Poulet's student was a bad student of Poulet would consist in the fact that Poulet could not identify with this student" (p. 85). Because the work's consciousness supersedes its objective form, critical readings have to be validated by intersubjective identification.

This abandonment of form worries Krieger in the essay that I started out discussing. In turning to Poulet, I have been trying not only to illustrate the antiformalist position that alarms Krieger but also to highlight the analogy between a literary text and a human being (between reading texts and knowing people) that pervades this discussion. Krieger concedes to Poulet—in terms that should by now be expected—that the New Criticism's endless explication of isolated literary texts has turned "the living body of the poems" into a "corpse," reducing the critic's role to "the pseudo-scientific one of post-mortem, dissection become autopsy" (p. 1232). Poulet's work accordingly represents an understandable, even inevitable, attempt "to restore life to literature, to reassert the critic as midwife instead of as coroner" (p. 1232). Krieger further grants Poulet that the abstractness of words threatens the particularity, spontaneity, and life of the person trying to use them. But for Krieger poetry—in fact, only poetry—miraculously defies the conventionality that stultifies other discourse. As the sole "immediate object," a poem somehow fuses eloquence and silence, reference and autonomy, life and structure, the intelligible and the sensible, subjectivity and form, motion and stillness, time and space, inner experience and outward expression, openness and closure. Because of poetry, we no longer have to choose, as Poulet thinks we must, between the ineffably subjective and the inertly objective. The "unique body" of the poems becomes our one way of using words to flesh out, and not just to veil, our thinking.

In Krieger, as in the New Criticism generally, the literary text does not simply benefit from the mind's intelligibility but establishes it. Apart from poetry, in everyday life, "to keep going as social animals," we presumably shy away from looking "too deeply into mirrors or into another's eyes" (p. 1249). But in poetry we break through the verbal evasions and barriers that we hide behind elsewhere. In poetry our formulas for avoidance, the polite, meaningless words that conceal us, give way to living forms of self-expression. Understandably (from Krieger's point of view) disenchanted with the formalists' sterile fixation on form, Poulet pushes interpretation toward mental telepathy, one disembodied consciousness somehow tapping into another. Krieger, by contrast, pictures reading as two incarnate beings—the reader and the text—meeting, not despite their bodies but because of them.

THE DEATH OF THE POEM IN MILLER, DE MAN, AND DERRIDA

In recent critiques of the New Criticism, the special literary object, already a miracle in Krieger, seems too good to be true. The oxymoronic terms that Krieger tries to keep together in the poem, while allowing for their divergence elsewhere, come apart, infecting even poetry with the emptiness that Krieger sees in other uses of language. The antimediating positions criticized by Krieger prefigure these later attacks by opposing the opaque surface, or objective form, of the text to its indeterminate interior dimension. In Derridean deconstruction, this interior dimension turns out to be indeterminate with a vengeance. Instead of a living body infused with meaning and consciousness, the text becomes a hollow shell or corpse, to use only two of many current metaphors for the now lifeless literary work. In discussing these metaphors, I will be sticking to some well-known texts, among them Miller's essays on Poulet, Wordsworth, and Stevens, de Man's *Blindness and Insight,* and Derrida's *Of Grammatology.* I choose these examples not despite their familiarity but because of it. They show that something resembling other-minds skepticism partly motivates deconstruction and shapes what remain its most influential texts.

Miller's "Geneva or Paris? The Recent Work of Georges Poulet," published in 1970, shows how deconstruction veers away not only from Poulet's criticism of consciousness but also from Krieger's refurbished contextualist alternative. In Poulet, as Miller astutely depicts him, reading allows us to recapture the author's immediate presence to himself, for Poulet the prelinguistic origin of literary texts. Against this meeting of minds, Miller opposes numerous developments in different disciplines that were beginning to become important in American deconstructive criticism: in particular, the contention of Emile Benveniste and, before him, Nietzsche that far from creating language, consciousness is a verbal creation, a linguistic rather than ontological term; Saussure's view that instead of preexisting words, meaning arises from their endless interplay; Nietzsche's point that behind every purportedly solid beginning lies still another seemingly more solid one, leading to an infinite regress of origins no one of which we can specify as an authentic point of departure; Heidegger's related observation that time not only disrupts the mind's presence to itself but also all our attempts at completeness; and, finally, Derrida's dismantling the "living present" in all its forms. These developments ensure what Miller calls, following Emmanuel Levinas, "the radical otherness of the other person": "Another mind is so alien, so impenetrable, that it is never possible by any means [literary or otherwise] to lift the veil which hides the other from me. This means that I can never confront the other person as an immediate presence, only encounter indirect signs and traces of his passage."[7] More radically, our failure to encounter the other person parallels the other's inability to grasp himself either in literature or apart from it. A poem, in short, is neither a self-sufficient, translucent object, as Krieger maintains, nor a means of insight into a consciousness that transcends language, as Poulet insists. Inside as well as outside literature, consciousness is not the source of words but their forever unstable product.

·Much of Miller's subsequent work embellishes the attitude toward consciousness and language that I have been describing. I will cite only two examples here: his reading of the dream of the Arab in book 5 of *The Prelude* and his commentary on Wallace Stevens's "The Rock," both from *The Linguistic Moment.* As Miller points out, Wordsworth pictures nature as a text or human body, frequently as an expressive, sometimes speaking face. In *The Prelude,* for instance, he looks

> Upon the speaking face of earth and heaven
> As her [the mind's] prime teacher, intercourse with
>   man
> Established by the sovereign Intellect,
> Who through that bodily image hath diffused,
> As might appear to the eye of fleeting time,
> A deathless spirit.
> (*The Prelude,* 5:13–18)

For Wordsworth, the sovereign intelligence expressed in natural forms is analogous to the human intelligence expressed not only in gestures and speech but in writing, usually in documents but sometimes on stones, trees, and other natural forms. These texts permit the dialogue of the mind with itself as well as communication with others. In the dream of the Arab, Wordsworth laments that man's means of expression—his books as well as his body—appear fragile in comparison with nature's, those everlasting natural forms that Wordsworth consistently depends on. In Miller's reading, the vulnerability and externality of man's media make writing an ominous necessity, something that in a better world we could dispense with:

> The mind of man in order to communicate with itself [and with others] must separate itself from itself, project itself into the external and mediate [not to mention fragile] form of books. The mind must divide its oneness into the multiplicity of signs stamped on the printed page, add to its natural power the supplementary power of the written word. In heaven we shall need neither book nor body, those garments of the soul, but as long as we are children of the earth we cannot go naked. (LM, 87)

For Miller, the dependency of the mind on writing turns out to indict not only the mind's natural power but also the sovereign intellect presumably housed in nature. In a series of reversals, the vulnerability of books exposes the vulnerability of our bodies as well as of those natural forms that at first seemed so expressive and solid. The following doubt insinuates itself in Wordsworth's poetry despite his efforts to ward it off: perhaps those natural forms do not manifest some divine intellect but only temporarily allow us to invent the illusion that one is there; perhaps instead of discovering meaning, we project it on the landscape as well as on others. The speaking face of the earth may be as unstable, as subject to time and to doubt, as the lines of poetry on a rock or the traces of a smile on a face.

An incident from the Arab's dream clarifies what is at stake here. The dreamer hears in a shell "a loud prophetic blast" in "an unknown tongue" that he can somehow "understand" (*The Prelude*, 5:93–95). As Miller points out, this sound, along with the flutings of the shell, recalls the "inscriptions apparently written by God on nature" (LM, 98). Although seeming to confirm the intelligibility of nature, the sound of the shell makes the language of God questionable because, Miller explains, the roar in the shell is in fact the listener's own blood beating in his ear. Instead of issuing from a single voice, moreover, the "loud prophetic blast" comes from a cacophonous multiplicity of "voices more than all the winds" (*The Prelude*, 5:107) that must be simplified to be heard as speech. The harmonious voice allegedly heard in the shell is thus neither as objective nor as univocal as Wordsworth would want. As the creation of the listener, the sound partakes of the finitude as well as the equivocality of all man's creations.

The life of a poem, the intelligibility of people, and the design of nature thus all take on a new, unwanted vulnerability in this episode. Objects, whether texts, natural forms, or bodies, at first appear to secure meaning by making it visible. But these same objects also threaten meaning. Their blankness, like the emptiness of the shell, makes meaning seem only our projection; the mutability of these objects similarly exposes meaning to the death that Wordsworth relies on material media to forestall. In this world at least, we cannot do without signs, lest we cut off communication and introspection. Yet we cannot do with signs what we want, namely, anchor consciousness in some intelligible, indestructible realm. Put more strongly, the very texts that allow for the appearance of meaning also kill it, or acknowledge its vanishing in our inevitable attempt to record it. As Miller points out, "Any poem means death, the imminent approach of death, but it is also dead. It is the corpse of its meaning, the spirit turned letter, mute marks on paper. The poem on the page is a dead body" (LM, 105). In the dream episode, although the Arab buries books to save them, his action ironically underscores their death. As Miller concludes, all texts end up being epitaphs—corpses, relics, stones, and empty shells that nullify the spiritual life that we necessarily call on them to protect.

The attempt to preserve consciousness in words suffers a similar fate in Miller's reading of Stevens's "The Rock." According to Miller, in trying to decipher the meaning of a poem, we often look for a "personal voice and a personal drama," in this case Stevens himself in old age. We want our reading to have "the security and enclosure of an intersubjective relation" (LM, 410), the sort of dialogue of one mind with another that Krieger and Poulet in different ways find in literature. In such a relation, Miller continues, "My self as reader would respond through the words to the self of the poet and communicate with him beyond the grave" (LM, 410). But the self in Stevens's poem turns out to be "baseless." It exists, but "in the same fragile and groundless way" as other arbitrary figures and images, "vanishing itself if they vanish" (LM, 413). This "abyssing or dissolution of the self" comes about in Stevens not when the self tries to withdraw from others but when it tries to found itself on a relation with another self. Stevens's poem, as Miller reads it, tracks the desire to "live in the houses of mothers," a sanctuary that supposedly nurtured a self that now feels lost and divided. According to Miller, this desire to do away with distance—from "the houses of mothers," from each other, and from ourselves—must remain unsatisfied. "The division perpetuates itself in whatever expedients are chosen to close or cure the wound," even such expedients as friendship and love. As Miller explains:

> In "a fantastic consciousness" (line 14) I face my sister self, that other desperate clod. I see in her a substitute for the lost mother, but the failure of that substitution reminds me that the mother was herself the abyss I have forgotten. The warmth in the mother's house was an illusion, something that never was. Her house stands "rigid in rigid emptiness" (line 6). My narcissistic relation to my double of the other sex is an affective movement seeking to find a bedrock for the self or in the self. It discovers only a perspective that begins again at B, a perpetually receding horizon. . . . The relation to my mirror image doubles my relation, across a generation gap, to my mother and reveals that relation, too, to have been an empty image, an icon of nothing. Though it seemed an enclosure, solidly based, it was already the abyss, since there was something missing that was suppressed or veiled. . . . Both the relation to the mother and the relation to the beloved are the experience of a perpetual distance, desire, dissatisfaction, an "emptiness that would be filled." (LM, 417–18)

Both the relation to the mother and the relation to the be-
loved, Miller concludes, are thus "figures, not realities"
(LM, 418).

In the comments by Miller that I have been citing, the
radical otherness of poems goes hand in hand with the radical otherness of people. Miller pictures the unintelligibility
of people and texts in various ways—as a distance we cannot traverse, a veil we cannot lift, a barrier we cannot penetrate, and a wound that will not close. Efforts to bridge this
gap (or set aside this veil)—friendship, love, poetry itself—necessarily fail or, what is the same thing, become
desperate expedients, tokens of our vain desire for com-
panionship, for the security and certitude of an intersubjective relationship. Commenting in another essay on *The
Triumph of Life*, Miller suggests that "lovemaking" attempts
to achieve wordlessly the same communion with another
that poetry seeks. Lovemaking turns out to be still another
way

> to "experience," as incarnate suffering, the self-de-
> structive effects of signmaking, signprojecting, and
> signinterpretation. The wordlessness of lovemaking
> is only another way of dwelling within signs after
> all. . . . [L]ovemaking is never a purely wordless com-
> munion or intercourse. It is in its turn contaminated by
> language. Lovemaking is a way of living, in the flesh,
> the aporias of figure. It is also a way of experiencing
> the way language functions to forbid the perfect union
> of lovers.[8]

Despite our wishes, the other, whether a poem or a person,
remains forever inscrutable—a blankness that we cannot decipher; a welter of merely indirect traces, confusing sounds,
and equivocal signs that we cannot sort through; a dead
body that will not come to life; mute marks that will not
become legible; a forever-vanishing illusion that we can
never pin down. From this point of view, we are as inacces-
sible to ourselves as we are to others: we cannot know ourselves apart from the problematic signs that come between
us and others. We exist, Miller says, but in the same fragile
and elusive way as the lines of a frown or poem.

Paul de Man reaches a similar conclusion, especially in *Blindness and Insight*, which starts the argument with Poulet's phenomenological criticism that Miller picks up in "Geneva or Paris?" In "Criticism and Crisis" (1969), de Man explains that recent Continental criticism

> represents a methodologically motivated attack on the notion that a literary or poetic consciousness is in any way a privileged consciousness, whose use of language can pretend to escape, to some degree, from the duplicity, the confusion, the untruth that we take for granted in the everyday use of language. We know that our entire social language is an intricate system of rhetorical devices designed to escape from the direct expression of desires that are, in the fullest sense of the term, unnameable—not because they are ethically shameful (for this would make the problem a very simple one), but because unmediated expression is a philosophical impossibility. (BI, 9)

This passage seems at first to criticize everyday discourse for evading or obstructing the direct expression of our desires. If we avoided these desires out of shame or reticence, de Man continues, the problem would be the "very simple one" of presumably facing up to them, becoming honest, and shedding our guilt or embarrassment. But unmediated expression of desire (or anything else, for that matter) is a philosophical impossibility. The confusion and duplicity that infect everyday language accordingly contaminate all attempts at authentic communication, even literature, which is often privileged (by Krieger, for example) as being the one place where we can rectify the dishonesty that prevails elsewhere. What seems to de Man an easy ethical or literary problem—overcoming the shallowness of everyday talk—turns out to be a philosophical impossibility, given the necessarily mediated, hence duplicitous, nature of all discourse.

Applying this view of language first to anthropology and then to literary criticism, de Man goes on to note that

> in the act of anthropological intersubjective interpretation, a fundamental discrepancy always prevents the observer [i.e., the anthropologist] from coinciding

fully with the consciousness that he is observing. The same discrepancy exists in everyday language, in the impossibility of making the actual expression coincide with what has to be expressed, of making the actual sign coincide with what it signifies. It is the distinctive privilege of language to be able to hide meaning behind a misleading sign, as when we hide rage or hatred behind a smile. But it is the distinctive curse of all language, as soon as any kind of interpersonal relation is involved, that it is forced to act this way. The simplest of wishes cannot express itself without hiding behind a screen of language that constitutes a world of intricate intersubjective relationships, all of them potentially inauthentic. In the everyday language of communication, there is no a priori privileged position of sign over meaning or of meaning over sign; the act of interpretation will always again have to establish this relation for the particular case at hand. The interpretation of everyday language is a Sisyphean task, a task without end and without progress, for the other is always free to make what he wants differ from what he says he wants. (BI, 11)

As in the preceding passage, an ethical option hardens into a philosophical inevitability. At first glance, we are free or privileged to mask our feelings behind words, to tell a helpless observer, "That is not what I meant at all. That is not it, at all." But this freedom turns out to be a curse laid on us, again, by the impossibility of making any expression match what we want to express. Instead of a transparent medium, language resembles a dense screen that we have to hide behind even when we may think we do not want to.

Far from remedying the inauthenticity of language, literature for de Man highlights it: "For the statement about language, that sign and meaning can never coincide, is what is precisely taken for granted in the kind of language we call literary. Literature, unlike everyday language, begins on the far side of this knowledge, it is the only form of language free from the fallacy of unmediated expression" (BI, 17)— free not because writers achieve unmediated expression but because they acknowledge its impossibility. In "The Literary Self as Origin: The Work of Georges Poulet" (1969), de Man elaborates on the view of reading that results. In theory, as I have shown, Poulet pictures reading as a secure interpersonal relationship or act of identification between the reader and the consciousness presiding over the text as its source. But in practice, de Man suggests, Poulet's criticism plunges us into a "process that, far from being the inexorable development of an impulse that none could resist, appears as extremely vulnerable, likely to go astray at any moment, always threatened with error and aberration, risking paralysis or self-destruction, and forever obliged to start again on the road that it had hoped to have covered" (BI, 97). This unsteady, endless process describes the growth of the writer's consciousness—the very consciousness that Poulet wants to make the already-formed, solid origin of the literary text. According to de Man, the jagged progress of the writer's self-creation results from its unavoidable dependence on language. Without language, the self cannot take shape; in de Man's words, the self "does not possess the power to engender its own duration" (BI, 100). But with language, "one runs the risk of hiding the self" (BI, 100), losing it in the confusion and mendacity endemic to words. While Poulet concedes the importance of language, he nevertheless must distrust it; hence, "the tone of anguish that inhabits the whole of his work and expresses a constant solicitude for literary survival. The subject that speaks in the criticism of Georges Poulet [de Man means both Poulet and the literary consciousness Poulet is trying to represent] is a vulnerable and fragile subject whose voice can never become established as a presence" (BI, 101).

In "The Rhetoric of Temporality," another one of the immensely influential essays gathered in *Blindness and Insight*, de Man leaves us with the following picture of our relation to language. In what he calls "everyday, common existence," language serves as a tool for getting things done. Sanity requires that we go along with the game of using language in ordinary, pragmatic ways, despite the dependency of everyday discourse on what de Man regards as "conventions of duplicity and dissimulation" that cover up "the inherent violence of the actual relationships between human beings" (BI, 215–16). In "acts of reflection" (in literature,

say, or philosophy), language allows us to distance ourselves from everyday life, transporting the social or empiri-
cal self into a textual world "constituted out of, and in,
language" (BI, 213). Although a writer's textual self at first
seems more authentic than the everyday one, for de Man it
is not. Unmasking the madness and hypocrisy that pass for
sanity does not cure us of our delusions, as in some "kind
of therapy" (BI, 216), but leaves us helpless to rectify them,
presumably because language again prohibits unmediated,
demystified self-expression or self-knowledge:

> The ironic, twofold self that the writer or philosopher
> constitutes by his language seems able to come into
> being only at the expense of his empirical self, falling
> (or rising) from a stage of mystified adjustment [pre-
> sumably to the duplicitous conventions of everyday
> life] into the knowledge of his mystification. The ironic
> language splits the subject into an empirical self that
> exists in a state of inauthenticity and a [literary] self
> that exists only in the form of a language that asserts
> the knowledge of this inauthenticity. This does not,
> however, make it into an authentic language [an au-
> thentic language being for de Man a contradiction in
> terms], for to know inauthenticity is not the same as to
> be authentic. (BI, 214)

Literary acts of reflection thus leave us aware of our everyday duplicity but unable to do anything about it. Language,
the cause of our evasiveness and dissembling, cannot be
their cure, not even in literature.

From the point of view de Man is taking in these early
essays, we turn out to be not simply unknown to one another and to ourselves but unknowable, not hiding behind
words but forever hidden.[9] In de Man's own words:

> The moment the innocence or authenticity of our sense
> of being in the world is put into question, a far from
> harmless process gets underway. It may start as a ca-
> sual bit of play with a stray loose end of the fabric,
> but before long the entire texture of the self is unrav-
> eled and comes apart. The whole process happens at
> an unsettling speed. Irony possesses an inherent ten-
> dency to gain momentum and not to stop until it has

run its full course; from the small and apparently in-
nocuous [even potentially therapeutic] exposure of a
small self-deception it soon reaches the dimensions of
the absolute. (BI, 215)

Instead of overcoming dissimulation, poets discover its absolute intractability. The velocity of this discovery—a stray,
loose end of the fabric unraveling the entire texture of the
self at unsettling speed—recalls the precipitousness of external-world skepticism, where the world disappears with
the generic object.

Derrida's early work parallels the line of thought that I
have been following in Miller and de Man. *Speech and Phenomena* (1967), for example, takes up the critique of phe-
nomenology that I have already noted in the essays by
Miller and de Man on Poulet, and "Signature Event Context," read as a paper in 1971, suspiciously probes the very
possibility of communication.[10] These works—and others I
need not cite—have been endlessly paraphrased, disputed,
and defended by numerous critics. Instead of reviewing
them still another time, I want here to discuss their bearing
on the problem of knowing other minds.

This problem, implicit everywhere in Derrida, is particularly important to *Of Grammatology*, which in part traces the
commitment of Jean Jacques Rousseau, Ferdinand de Saussure, Claude Lévi-Strauss, and other thinkers to speech (as
opposed to writing). When contrasted to writing, speech
from the point of view of these thinkers seems more immediate, powerful, direct, full, alive, natural, and internal, inseparable from the very breath and being of the person
speaking. Considered from the perspective of the listener,
Derrida writes, voice "penetrates into me violently, it is the
privileged route for forced entry and interiorization."[11] I
can more easily close my eyes to something at a distance
than shut my ears to something nearby. Speech appeals to
these writers because it consequently secures presence—
"self-presence" as well as community, or what Rousseau
and Lévi-Strauss describe as the face-to-face presence of
people to each other within earshot, assembled in their
own neighborhood. In place of living, authentic speech,
writing substitutes mute, impersonal signs that leave intact

the distance they are meant to overcome. By destroying "the co-presence of citizens, the unanimity of 'assembled peoples,'" writing creates, or ratifies, what Derrida, paraphrasing Rousseau, calls "a situation of dispersion, holding subjects so far apart as to be incapable of feeling themselves together in the space of one and the same speech, one and the same persuasive exchange" (OG, 137).

The second half of *Of Grammatology* follows Rousseau's tortuous struggle to protect presence or, what becomes the same thing, to keep speech free of the dangerous inauthenticity that infects not only writing but other surrogates for genuine presence, among them such initially surprising analogues for writing as masturbation and representative government. Each of these substitutes poses as a possibly inoffensive, maybe even beneficial, supplement to some presumably fuller or more natural term—speech in the case of writing (writing adds to speech by extending in space and time its power to secure presence); sexual intercourse in the case of masturbation (masturbation makes up for a temporarily absent presence, immediately procuring this absent presence, Derrida says, through its image); and community in the case of representative government (political representatives stand in for, or signify, the people in their absence). These substitutes are admittedly risky; instead of restoring presence or only occasionally compensating for its absence, they may tempt us into preferring the illusion or sign to the real thing. But Rousseau apparently desires these substitutes even as he fears their attenuation of presence.

Derrida shows how the very need for such supplements exposes a lack in what they supplement—a lack Rousseau does not want to acknowledge—thus generating a series of substitutions that neither begins nor ends in a positive term. "Through this sequence of supplements," Derrida explains, "a necessity is announced: that of an infinite chain, ineluctably multiplying the supplementary mediations that produce the sense of the very thing they defer: the mirage of the thing itself, of immediate presence, of originary perception. Immediacy is derived" (OG, 157). Rousseau wants to separate the presence of individuals to one another in sexual intercourse, say, from a merely ancillary, solitary substitute like masturbation. But according to Derrida, instead of following or terminating in some presumably fuller experience, masturbation produces the very sense of reality that Rousseau wants it to assist. This sense of a more natural or real experience is an illusion and is forever beyond our reach, no matter what measures we take to attain it. Anticipating Miller's remark on lovemaking mentioned earlier, Derrida concludes that each new step toward presence turns out to be still another inadequate substitute for presence, reproducing the emptiness we want to overcome. According to Derrida, "we are thus dispossessed of the longed-for presence in the gesture of language by which we attempt to seize it" (OG, 141).

In Derrida's analysis, the limits of sexual intercourse—its kinship with the image-dependent onanism that Rousseau wishes to place beneath it—reappear in conversation, pity, love, community, and every other attempt to appropriate, or reappropriate, presence. Rousseau pictures conversation as a conduit or medium transmitting a meaning that remains untouched. More exactly, in Derrida's words, conversation from Rousseau's point of view is "a communication between two absolute origins that, if one may venture the formula, auto-affect reciprocally, repeating as immediate echo the auto-affection produced by the other" (OG, 166). The other's presence to himself—his direct experience of happiness, say—is immediately "echoed" in my awareness of his experience. According to Derrida, "immediacy is here the myth of consciousness" (OG, 166). We are no more immediately present to ourselves than we are to others because all experience is always already mediated by language, even supposedly direct or "personal" experience. The words, gestures, and expressions used by one person in communicating with another neither threaten some prior meaning (here, our supposedly pure, original experience of happiness) nor successfully convey it without loss. In Derrida's words, "the supplementary sign does not expose to death by affecting a self-presence that is already possible. *Auto*-affection constitutes the same (*auto*) as it divides the same. Privation of presence is the condition of experience, that is to say of presence" (OG, 166). The dialogue of my mind with itself is as "fissured," as victimized by "the opacity and indirectness of the signifier," as any attempt at conversation with someone else. "No one," Derrida concludes, "is there for anyone, not even for himself" (OG, 233).

Pity and love are as disappointing as conversation. Rousseau grounds pity and love in the relationship between mother and child, especially in the mother's reassuring "soft voice," an important means of her natural, "maternal solicitude." Pity is thus on the side of life (here, the preservation of the species), presence (the mother's being there for the child), and voice (the mother's comforting song), a familiar constellation of terms in Rousseau. Rousseau goes on to suggest that imagination, not reason, necessarily activates natural pity. As Derrida puts it, paraphrasing Rousseau, "when pity is awakened itself by imagination and reflection, when sensible presence is exceeded by its image, we can imagine and judge that the other feels and suffers" (OG, 189). Conversely, in Rousseau's own words, "He who imagines nothing senses no-one but himself; he is alone in the midst of humankind" (quoted in OG, 187). In imagining someone else's suffering, we still see it as someone else's. We consequently pity others while keeping our distance from them. We distance ourselves not, Rousseau emphasizes, out of selfishness but out of a desirable love of self. "In the experience of suffering as the suffering of the other," Derrida comments, "the imagination, as it opens us to a certain nonpresence within presence, is indispensable: the suffering of others is lived by comparison, as our nonpresent, past or future suffering," even, Derrida suggests earlier, as the sign of our own eventual death (OG, 191).

In Derrida's reading, the link between pity and imagination turns out to be dangerous as well as necessary. Imagination undermines the relationship with the other that it facilitates; in Derrida's formulation, it breeches the unity that it broaches. The opposite of pity is fear, a reaction to what Derrida describes as "a situation of threat, distress, and dereliction, to an archaic solitude, to the anguish of dispersion" (OG, 277). Rousseau provides one such situation in the *Essay on the Origin of Languages* when he writes of a savage man who is so initially frightened by others that he calls them giants. Correcting this mistake—substituting "man," for instance, for "giant" or even learning the man's proper name—only perpetuates the estrangement it would remedy. Designed to overcome space and bridge differences, language is spaced and differential. Naming itself is violent: in Derrida's words, to name "is the originary violence of language which consists in inscribing within a difference, in classifying, in suspending the vocative absolute. To think the unique [self] within the system [of language], to inscribe it there, such is the gesture of the arche-writing, arche-violence, loss of the proper, of absolute proximity, of self-presence, in truth the loss of what has never taken place, of a self-presence which has never been given but only dreamed of and always already split, repeated, incapable of appearing to itself [or to others] except in its own disappearance" (OG, 112). The inexorable law of the supplement is again at work here, turning the apparent progression in intimacy from "giant" to "man" into a frustrating lateral movement that can never end. Humanizing the other, identifying with him, and exchanging pity for fear only perpetuate his nonpresence or, what is the same thing for Derrida, the dependency on language and imagination of his fitful presence to me. As Derrida typically puts it, even the mother's soothing voice—to go back to a seemingly more secure relationship—is thus riddled, furrowed, contaminated, infected, and corrupted with everything that Rousseau wants to put outside it: difference, signification, and spacing, with death itself inhabiting the dead spaces that fracture what she says.

Derrida suggests that Rousseau focuses on pity and fear in part because of their classical link with the theater, especially with tragedy. As mentioned earlier, in valuing speech, Rousseau, like Lévi-Strauss, upholds a certain kind of society—a community of free-speaking individuals authentically present to one another. He accordingly opposes what Derrida calls a theatrical society, that is, a society bound up with spectacle, rhetoric, representation, masks, scripts, imitation, pretense, convention, playacting, spectatorship (as opposed to involvement), and interpretation. Although Rousseau fears the world becoming a stage in Paris, say, or in the modern period, Derrida implies that it always already is one. In Rousseau's own writings we are consequently "always short of or beyond" (OG, 267) the idyllic community that he longs for. Far from signaling deprivation, a "theatrical society" becomes redundant in Derrida's analysis. Reliant on imagination, rhetoric, and nonpresent images, pity and fear are staged outside as well as inside the theater.[12]

Like Miller and de Man, Derrida in *Of Grammatology* thus does not so much turn texts into especially open people as people into indecipherable texts. Commenting on his own reading of Rousseau, Derrida remarks, "*There is nothing outside of the text*" (OG, 158) and not simply because we have access to the "real" Rousseau only through his writing. "All reasons of this type would already be sufficient," Derrida notes, "but there are more radical reasons" (OG, 158) bearing on all human relationships, not just on our relationship to a deceased writer. Even in what

> one calls the real life of these existences of "flesh and bone," beyond and behind what one believes can be circumscribed as Rousseau's text, there has never been anything but writing; there have never been anything but supplements, substitutive significations which could only come forth in a chain of differential references, the "real" supervening, and being added only while taking on meaning from a trace and from an invocation of the supplement, etc. And thus to infinity, for we have read, *in the text* [i.e., Rousseau's writings], that the absolute present, Nature, that which words like "real mother" name, have always already escaped, have never existed; that what opens meaning and language is writing as the disappearance of natural presence. (OG, 159)

Words like "real mother" invoke a presence that has never existed. Derrida challenges us to imagine a more direct way to the "real Rousseau" presumably hidden behind his writings—talking to him, for example, for an hour, a semester, or even ten years. The arbitrariness of whatever time we put here indicates the futility of our efforts. Each allegedly more immediate or profound contact with Rousseau only substitutes for a still more immediate or profound encounter that we desire but can never achieve. Every attempt to reach the flesh-and-blood Rousseau pushes "him" away, with "him" typically demanding quotation marks because "he" may not be there in the first place. Instead of limiting his texts, the disappearance of the real Rousseau is accordingly inseparable from them. "He" is a function of our desire for some end (or beginning) to our interpretative labor. "Representation *in the abyss* of presence is not an accident of presence" brought about, for example, by the subject's death or temporary absence; "the desire for presence is, on the contrary, born from the abyss (the indefinite multiplication) of representation, from the representation of representation," never from the representation of some stable extralinguistic referent. From Derrida's point of view, "there is not, strictly speaking, a text whose author or subject is Jean Jacques Rousseau" (p. 246).[13]

Our difficulties in turning aside or penetrating Rousseau's writings to reach the "real Rousseau" parallel "Rousseau's" own difficulties in seizing or shaping himself. Derrida frequently pictures Rousseau struggling with language, trying to say one thing only to end up saying another. Rousseau wants to say, for instance, that writing supplements speech in the benign sense of extending the power of speech to establish presence. But "supplement" sabotages his intention, laying bare a deficiency in speech that he does not want to see. "His declared intention is not annulled by this but rather *inscribed* within a system it no longer dominates" (OG, 243)—inscribed as an ultimately futile desire to tame language, to keep in check its corrosion of all claims of presence.[14] Despite Rousseau's wishes, language is finally an unruly force, even a "machine of death" (OG, 301), death to the self that the writer would express by means of it.[15] As Derrida puts it, "the indefinite process of supplementarity has always already *infiltrated* presence, always already inscribed there the space of repetition and the splitting of the self" (OG, 163), a split that neither writer nor reader can heal.

Labeling writing a machine would seem to take us full circle by reintroducing the mechanistic metaphors that the New Critics' organicism, and before that Coleridge's Romanticism, tried to resist. (De Man's rehabilitating allegory at the expense of the symbol also seems at first glance to reinstate a pre-Romantic aesthetic.) Equating deconstruction with mechanism and Romanticism with organicism in this way of course oversimplifies things. Even so, Derrida, de Man, and Miller, in criticizing expressive views of literature, do picture language as a brute force waylaying the helpless self, like a machine dominating its would-be user. As I suggested earlier, predeconstructive critics like Krieger and Poulet allow for the loss or avoidance of self-expression in extraliterary writing, say, or in everyday talk. But for these critics literature can still cut through the evasiveness that prevails elsewhere. In different ways, Miller, de Man, and Derrida take away this privilege not only from literature but from anything else we might imagine as more direct or expressive. Knowing other minds and even knowing our own mind consequently become problems that nothing will solve, much as in Cavell's characterization of other-minds skepticism, to which I now turn.

CAVELL ON READING OTHER MINDS

Although the problem of other minds mostly occupies part 4 of *The Claim of Reason*, it briefly appears in part 1, a discussion of Wittgenstein, criteria, and human knowledge. Cavell is using Wittgenstein to highlight what both men regard as the remarkable depth of our agreement with one another, our "mutual attunement" in concepts, values, and judgments. What makes this attunement so

> astonishing, what partly motivates [Wittgenstein's] philosophizing on the subject, is that the extent of agreement is so intimate and pervasive; that we communicate in language as rapidly and completely as we do; and that since we cannot assume that the words we are given have their meaning by nature, we are led to assume they take it from convention; and yet no current idea of "convention" could seem to do the work that words do—there would have to be, we could say, too many conventions in play, one for each shade of each word in each context. We *cannot* have agreed beforehand to all that would be necessary. (CR, 31)[16]

In this passage, intimacy is not so much an achievement or something we have had to struggle for as it is a remarkable fact—remarkable because nothing seems to account for it, not nature (the meaning of our words is culturally rather than naturally, or divinely, determined) but not convention either (our mutual attunement is too intricate and extensive to have resulted from some merely convenient, arbitrary agreement).

Cavell's starting from the fact of our intimacy puts him at odds with literary critics like Krieger as well as with Derrida, Miller, and de Man. Instead of reserving intimacy for literary communication, Cavell makes intimacy an everyday achievement, a matter of our constantly sharing feelings, interests, values, judgments, and concepts. Similarly, whereas de Man and Derrida stress the impossibility of our being present to one another, Cavell emphasizes the astonishing reality of our attunement. De Man's picture of human communication centers around the anthropologist—the detached, puzzled outsider—observing and necessarily failing to decipher an alien culture. Cavell's model suggests two people effortlessly exchanging something, a joke, for example, or a grievance. The velocity of the exchange impresses Cavell as much as the rapid unraveling of the self strikes de Man. Finally, for de Man, language, "as soon as any interpersonal relation is involved" (BI, 11), condemns us to duplicity. Cavell, by contrast, always implicates language in interpersonal relationships; learning words as well as using them involves us with others.

This starting point—the depth of our mutual attunement—motivates Cavell's thinking about other-minds skepticism. Instead of obviating other-minds skepticism, our attunement explains it. More specifically, in light of our intimacy, other-minds skepticism becomes a disturbing human possibility, or temptation.

In posing the problem of other minds (making knowledge of other minds a problem), the skeptic typically seizes on what he sees as our inability to be certain that someone else is experiencing a particular feeling—pain, for example, or sympathy. From this point of view, we are unable to be certain that the other person is in pain partly because we have to take his word for it (he could be lying or faking) and partly because we are never able in a particular situation to review all our criteria for his being in pain. We cannot always check that he flinches when someone touches the allegedly painful spot or that he constantly favors the supposedly injured limb, and so on.

Our difficulties here (in deciding whether the other person is really in pain) reinforce a more general feeling that we unfortunately have to get to the other's pain via a particular, conventional expression of pain, a groan, say, or a wince. As observers, we feel frustrated because instead of reaching the pain itself, we are restricted to observing merely indirect signs and superficial symptoms. In being conventional, or not natural, these signs can seem arbitrary: what we hear as a groan might be (to him) a song or a signal to a pet and not necessarily a sign of pain. Our means of expressing pain may only be ours: how can we be sure that they are his, or that he is not simply using them to trick us, perhaps to make us feel unwarranted sympathy or to lay bare our lack of concern?

The anxiety and uncertainty behind these questions are magnified when we confront a stranger, perhaps someone from an alien culture, as in the scenario mentioned by de Man. We may feel unable to decide on his (or its) humanity, let alone his really feeling (what we call) pain. For Cavell, this possibility, however important, only highlights the apprehensiveness we may feel every day because we have to decide in each case, at every moment, whether someone is in pain and we realize that there is nothing assured about such a judgment. Our frustration comes to a head when, as parents and teachers, we would initiate others in our form of life, for example by showing them how we express pain or when we respond to it. With a shock, we realize that all such instruction at some unforeseeable point must come to an end and that although we expect and want our pupil to go on (using words or reading poems and expressions a certain way, for example), we cannot force him, or rather we do not want to force him but want him to see the legitimacy of our procedures. Yet we feel unable to say enough on behalf of them, to get beneath them to some more solid ground (such as nature). Feeling powerless to persuade our would-be pupils, we discover how much of our way of life must be learned—and how little we can teach. In Cavell's words, "I am thrown back upon myself; I as it were turn my palms outward, as if to exhibit the kind of creature I am, and declare my ground occupied, only mine, ceding yours. When? When do I find or decide that the time has come to grant you secession, allow [or not allow] your divergence to stand, declare that the matter between us is at an end? The anxiety lies not just in the fact that my understanding *has* limits, but that I must *draw* them, on apparently no more ground than my own" (CR, 115).

Using these experiences (among others recorded in *The Claim of Reason*), the other-minds skeptic concludes that we cannot really know that someone else is in pain, to stay with the example that comes up most often in this discussion.[17] At most we can say, "I don't mind calling that pain" or "I guess that is pain" or "For all practical purposes—a trip to a doctor, say, or an insurance claim—that counts as pain." There is something chilling or at least guarded about such responses. When we hesitate calling that pain (because we cannot be sure), we also withhold ourselves from the other person—our sympathy, say, or our help. More strongly, we are not simply saying that we cannot know how it is with that creature.

> There is now nothing there, of the right kind, to be known. There is nothing to read from that body, nothing the body is *of*; it does not go beyond itself, it expresses nothing; it does not so much as behave. There is no body left to manifest consciousness (or unconsciousness). It is not dead, but inanimate; it hides nothing, but is absolutely at my disposal; if it were empty it would be quite hollow, but in fact it is quite dense, though less uniform than stone. . . . It does not matter to me now whether there turn out to be wheels and springs inside, or stuffing, or some subtler or messier mechanism; or rather, whether it matters depends [only] upon my curiosity in such matters. . . . My feeling is: What this "body" lacks is *privacy*. (CR, 84)

With such a "body," analogous in its lifelessness and inscrutability to the inanimate, deconstructed text described in the last section, my words lose their force and my signs their life. Skepticism, though meant to find others, ends up shutting them out by seeing them as terminally closed to me.

Cavell characteristically does not want to repudiate the skeptic's experience but to show how it comes about. In *The Claim of Reason*, denial, escape, and disappointment figure most prominently in Cavell's account of other-minds skepticism. "In making the knowledge of others a metaphysical difficulty," he writes, "philosophers deny how real the practical difficulty is of coming to know another person, and how little we can reveal of ourselves to another's gaze, or bear of it. Doubtless such denials are part of the motive which sustains metaphysical difficulties" (CR, 90). De Man provides an apt example of what I think Cavell has in mind here when he notes, in the passage cited earlier (BI, 9), that if shame obstructed our relationships with one another, then our problem would be "very simple." But the philosophical impossibility of unmediated expression turns an otherwise easy task (overcoming shame) into an insuperable one (breaking through the duplicity intrinsic to language). De Man's complacency toward shame here, his denying its considerable power, feeds his philosophical pessimism. The philosophical problem of unmediated expression seems difficult only when opposed to the apparently simple everyday one of letting ourselves be seen.

Cavell further suggests, following Wittgenstein, that the sense of a gap between us and others originates in our wishing to give up responsibility for maintaining those shared forms of life linking us to others. The Ancient Mariner's killing the albatross (in Coleridge's *The Rime of the Ancient Mariner*) provides Cavell with an unexpected example here. Noting that "the bird . . . loved the man / Who shot him with his bow," Cavell points out that the Mariner "may only have wanted at once to silence the bird's claim upon him and to establish a connection with it closer, as it were, than his caring for it: a connection beyond the force of his human responsibilities, whether conventional or personal, either of which can seem arbitrary" (IQO, 197). I imagine personal responsibilities here to include feeding the bird, caring for it, and maybe even talking to it, as people do with pets. These acts can seem arbitrary or based on superstition, say, rather than on any shared life with the bird. At least I think they seem this way to the ship's crew, which takes care of the bird only because taking care of it appears to make "the breeze to blow." (When, immediately after the Mariner kills the bird, the sun rises, the crew swears, "'Twas right . . . such birds to slay, / That bring the fog and mist." The progress of the ship, not the life of the bird, is clearly on the pragmatic mind of the crew.) Impatient with the crew's merely superstitious adoption of the bird, the Mariner would rather put the bird to death than feel shut out of its life or let in only by indirect, conventional means such as feeding it. It is as if the Mariner, like the other-minds skeptic, cannot tolerate his distance or separation from the bird and as if, in reaction to the discovery of this separateness, the Mariner inadvertently ends up perpetuating it, or radicalizing it, by putting the bird forever out of reach.

More generally, the skeptic's stepping outside ordinary-language games—the forms of life we share with others—at once results from and exacerbates the skeptic's sense that they are arbitrary, that their inevitable dependency on our abiding by them somehow lessens their authority. Faced with our responsibility for our forms of life, the skeptic begins to feel that they are too fragile, too much like particular agreements, and too dependent on the unpredictable assent of others. In skepticism, Cavell explains, "it is as though we try to get the world [and others] to provide answers in a way which is independent of our responsibility for *claiming* something to be so (to get God to tell us what we must do in a way which is independent of our responsibility for choice)" (CR, 216). In the case of pain or some other sensation, we again wish to reach the other's feeling apart from his expressing it or apart from our having to construe it, as if that were the only way to ensure certainty or candor.[18]

This uneasiness with the fact that our forms of life are ours again registers the skeptic's disappointment in them. From the skeptic's point of view, their lack of necessity, of natural or supernatural backing, subjects them to seemingly random change, among other things. A wave of the hand could signify friendship today and contempt tomorrow, or indifference next door. The fact that our criteria could have developed in any way subverts the particular way they have developed, making it seem accidental, merely convenient or even tyrannical, denying us the right to signify friendship, say, however we want. For the skeptic, Cavell writes, "if the a priori has a history"—and what we call a priori, natural, or necessary always does—"it cannot really be the a priori" (CR, 119).

By linking skepticism to denial (of the practical difficulty posed by intimacy), escape (from the language games that alone ensure our communicating with one another), and disappointment (with the apparent lack of necessity that tarnishes our criteria, stigmatizing them as merely ours), Cavell is trying to characterize skepticism, not to refute it. For him, there is no refuting it, anymore than there is human life without disappointment and desire. Throughout *The Claim of Reason,* he shows his respect for skepticism by criticizing several attempts to repudiate it. One is the argument by analogy, which asserts that we know others by comparison with ourselves. Commenting on Rousseau in a passage cited earlier, Derrida offers, then deconstructs, a version of this argument when he writes that "the suffering of others is lived by comparison, as our nonpresent, past or future suffering" (OG, 191). In the argument by analogy, we usually relate the other's behavior or body to our own, reasoning, for example, that because we are in pain when we flinch, the other is probably in pain, too. For Cavell, this argument, far from overturning skepticism, reproduces a picture of behavior that motivates skepticism. The hidden step in the argument is that the other is (merely) like us, at least on the outside, and that sentience or some other inner state has to be extrapolated from appearance. The gap between outer and inner here, between what we see and what we must infer or surmise, leaves an opening for skepticism instead of warding it off. In Derrida's terms, our having to infer suffering or imagine it only on the basis of what we presumably would feel creates a certain nonpresence within presence—a nonpresence (what we probably would feel) that puts in doubt the very presence it makes available (what the other feels). Instead of resurrecting Rousseau's weak argument by analogy against other-minds skepticism, Cavell lets it die.

Vanquishing skepticism by direct assertion is similarly unsuccessful. Cavell pictures a man standing up to stretch, grimacing in excruciating pain, then adding, "There is *something* here accompanying my whine of pain," perhaps in an effort to elicit the sympathy of his companions (CR, 337). In Cavell's analysis, the man's desperate, even mad insistence on these words breaks the connection between behavior (here, grimacing) and feeling (pain) that he wishes to make. (The man protests too much.) "Breaks the connection" suggests a connection already there that the man unwittingly snaps:

> The words "something accompanying my cry of pain" are forced upon us when we feel we must enforce the *connection* between something inner and an outer something. But those very words—or rather the insistence with which in such an eventuality they are employed, or the reservation with which they are withheld—exactly serve to break this natural connection. . . . They make the fact that an expression and what it expresses go together seem more or less accidental. (CR, 338)

If what Cavell calls our natural expressions of pain will not work, or if we nervously fail to let them work, then proclaiming "I'm really in pain" will only widen the gap between us and others that we want to close—the gap that our own words open up.

This anecdote, with its emphasis on the "natural" connection between an expression and what it expresses, returns me to the mutual attunement that I said motivated Cavell's thinking on other-minds skepticism. In addition to backfiring, the man's insistence here seems as unnecessary as adding "I really mean that I want the salt" after asking someone please to pass it. Communication does not ordinarily require such added, or anxious, effort. Even so, "natural" here cannot mean "necessary." A particular expression of pain is not the only one imaginable, as the skeptic rightly observes. Cavell concedes the conventionality of our expressions while appreciating their naturalness and efficacy in a given setting. Although we can imagine other ways of requesting the salt (our own way not being "natural" or necessary), in some contexts "please pass the salt" not only works but seems the best, maybe even the sole, thing to say.

The literary implications of what Cavell is saying here surface when he discusses our ability to read others as well as be read by them. According to Cavell, when facing other people, I have to read or interpret them—their gestures and expressions, what Wittgenstein would call their physiognomy, as well as their words. Multiple possibilities arise in reading others: my being wrong (my counting a grimace, for instance, as a smile), unsure, surprised (when an unexpected aspect of the other's physiognomy dawns on me), and aware of something I cannot prove, to name only a few.[19] In each case, I express my reading of others (as well as my reading of myself) by my attitude and by the position I take with respect to their history. Again there are numerous possibilities, including lack of interest in the other's story as well as suspicion and love.

Like the other-minds skeptic, I can feel shut out from someone else's life or hidden in my own, invisible (like Ralph Ellison's protagonist) or veiled by my body (to use one of Miller's metaphors). But for Cavell what comes between me and others is not the body but our employment of it—my (or the other's) blindness in reading it or my (or the other's) ineptitude in using it. Again the possibilities are limitless or only limited by something as supple as human nature. Failure to acknowledge others—to read them as human—may indicate not the absence of something in them but the presence of something in us: confusion, indifference, callousness, exhaustion, coldness, spiritual emptiness, among many other possibilities.[20] From Cavell's point of view, we are separate, as the skeptic insists. But we are nevertheless still responsible for everything that comes between us. If we can be blind to one another, we can also see (even sometimes see through) one another; if opaque to one another, also clear; if hidden, also open; and so on.

In reading others, we are proclaiming our "internal relation" to them—what I have called our attunement with them—or denying it. Cavell provides one especially important example of an attempt at connection—antiabortionists calling the foetus a human life—and another of an attempt at severance—slave owners trying to deny the humanity of slaves. For Cavell, the statement that the slave is not a human being, like the statement that the foetus is, cannot be fully meant. Everything in the slave owner's way of life with slaves shows his identification with them—his converting slaves (and not horses) to Christianity, say, or tipping a black driver instead of petting him. Similarly, the antiabortionists do not act as if killing foetuses were on a par with killing children but reserve more abhorrence for the latter. The slave owner really believes that some humans are slaves, not that slaves are subhumans. Although he may assert the latter, his attitude, again, shows that he cannot mean anything definite by it.

These examples are important because they show that knowledge—in particular, scientific knowledge—does not guarantee acknowledgment. The slave owner may know everything anyone may want to inform him about slaves in arguing for their humanity—their physical resemblance to their owners, their seemingly human skills and needs, their verbal abilities, and so on. None of these things necessarily counts as evidence of the slave's being human. Animals, dolls, and automatons can acquire many of these human traits, just as humans can lose them. At one point Cavell asks, "Why is it that we attach such extreme importance to the human guise, I mean form?" (CR, 393). The answer would seem to be that we do not, or do not always have to, in deciding on someone's humanity. "Being human is the power to grant being human. Something about flesh and blood elicits [or can elicit?] this grant from us, and something about flesh and blood can also repel it" (CR, 397). "Something" is deliberately vague here: Cavell refuses to let our humanity depend on a fixed set of physical traits or intellectual skills.

We can still argue with the slave owner, not by appealing to what he overlooks in slaves but by exposing what he avoids in himself—the gap between his claim (that slaves are not human) and his attitude (which suggests they are). When we try to deny the humanity of others—when we refuse to read them as human or when we declare ourselves

illegible to them—we withhold ourselves from them, sometimes out of fear, suspicion, and distrust. These feelings can
be well-founded. If we never had them, Cavell points out,
we would be like clowns, endlessly in love with the world,
yet always "up to being the one who gets slapped, to being
one for whom dignity does not depend on standing, to
be[ing] beyond expectation" (CR, 452). (Cavell has in mind
here what becomes of the clown on film, in particular the
work of Charlie Chaplin and Buster Keaton.)[21] The clown
seems beyond other feelings as well, such as horror (for
Cavell, our response to the precariousness of human identity, its vulnerability to being lost or not recognized); self-
consciousness (which can come between our consciousness
and our expression of it, making us feel, like Hamlet, as if
our expressions—in Hamlet's case, his "inky cloak," sighs,
tears, and "dejected havior of the visage"—were artificial or
merely conventional and "but the trappings and the suits of
woe," "actions that a man might play"); and embarrassment
(one thing we fear when we worry about whether others are
the human beings that we take them for, as, for example, in
the recent movie *Splash*, when the mortified lead character
discovers that the "woman" he has fallen in love with is really a mermaid. We don't want to repeat his mistake).

Most of us most of the time are not clowns, which is
a way of saying that we take into account the skepticism
about others that the clown transcends or sets aside. To
function in the world, as the skeptic concedes, we have to
act as if desks, envelopes, and so on exist: hence the limits
of external-world skepticism (for better or for worse, it stays
in the study). Being with others—playing backgammon or
billiards, dining with friends, and so on—offsets this form
of skepticism, making it seem cold, strained, and ridiculous
(in Hume's phrase), inseparable from the isolated thinking
that accompanies it. In other-minds skepticism, however,
being with others poses the problem; it cannot be the cure.
I accordingly live this form of skepticism and even feel compelled to respect its insights.

Living this form of skepticism does not, however, mean
being consumed by it. The skeptic's terminal doubt about
others is not the only alternative to the clown's blind faith.

We can be overtaken by suspicion—hence the possibility of tragedy, as I will be showing in my next chapter—but we do not have to be (making comedy also possible). If I can avoid others, I can also face them; if I can shut others out, I can also let them in. Cavell accordingly speaks of letting yourself matter to others, which for him means acknowledging

> that your expressions in fact express you, that they are yours, that you are in them. This means allowing yourself to be comprehended, something you can always deny. Not to deny it is, I would like to say, to acknowledge your body, and the body of your expressions, to be yours, you on earth, all there will ever *be* of you. (CR, 383)

Acknowledging others similarly involves taking their expressions as theirs, as them.

For Cavell, my taking or reading you as human depends on nothing more than what he calls my capacity for empathic projection: "I must settle upon the validity of my projection from within my present condition, from within, so to speak, my confinement from you. For there would be no way for me to step outside my projections" (CR, 423). "Projection" implies something coming from within me, some power to extend or deny humanity to someone else. (Being human, again, is the power to grant being human.) Others can reveal their humanity to me, but only if I let them, as the slave owner example suggests. For Cavell, "I must settle upon the validity of my projection"; there is no outside arbiter to whom I can pass off this responsibility. I might want an outsider to judge my projection of humanity on someone else—to answer the question, Is X really human? But such an outsider cannot answer this question without also judging my attribution of humanity to myself, that is, without deciding whether I know what "being human" means. According to Cavell, I cannot tolerate anyone being in a better position than I am in to determine my own humanity, not even God. (Why would I believe anyone who told me that I was not human?)[22] Putting myself off limits to an outsider undermines the outsider's authority, in effect making the outsider's vantage point equivalent to my own. Allowing the outsider to decide on my case, however, gives the outsider too much authority. I have to decide for myself whether I am correctly projecting humanity on someone else.

Moreover, I must decide on my projection "from within my present condition." There may be no better situation, no single best case for determining whether someone is human. In external-world skepticism, to get along in the world we have to forget that the best case for knowing objects fails us. In other-minds skepticism, we have to remember that we might here and now be in the best situation possible for knowing others.

> Mightn't it be that just this haphazard, unsponsored state of the world, just this radiation of relationships, of my cares and commitments, provides the milieu in which my knowledge of others can best be expressed? Just *this*—say expecting someone to tea; or returning a favor; waving goodbye; reluctantly or happily laying in groceries for a friend with a cold; feeling rebuked, and feeling it would be humiliating to admit the feeling; pretending not to understand that the other has taken my expression, with a certain justice, as meaning more than I sincerely wished it to mean; hiding inside a marriage; hiding outside a marriage—just such things are perhaps the most that knowing others comes to, or has come to for me. (CR, 439)

We are often disappointed in our occasions for knowing others and for expressing that knowledge, "as though we have, or have lost, some picture of what knowing another, or being known by another, would really come to—a harmony, a concord, a union, a transparence, a governance, a power—against which our actual successes at knowing, and being known, are poor things" (CR, 440). Again, our "actual successes at knowing and being known" seem "poor things" partly because they depend on our accepting seemingly arbitrary ways of communicating: our meaning, or letting, a wave to be seen as a gesture of friendship and a grimace to be taken as a sign of pain and, more generally, our acknowledging our expressions as ours, as us. But imagining better opportunities for relating to others can become a way of avoiding the ones at hand, avoiding them not because they conceal me but because they reveal me—my caring for others, my hiding from them, and my embarrassment before them, to name only a few of the possibilities mentioned in the passage above.

From Cavell's point of view, my everyday relationships with others are thus not confined, as de Man sees them, but exposed, and "not to possibilities but to actualities, to history" (CR, 432). For better or for worse, "there is no possibility of human relationship that has not been enacted. The worst has befallen, befalls every day" (CR, 432); so has the best. Being exposed to the best case, moreover, means that my attempts to restrict my relations with others or see them as restricted may collapse. My disclaimers, evasions, and excuses may fail, at any time, in any place, exposing what I want to hide.

I must thus decide on the validity of my projection of humanity on others from within my present circumstances, which for Cavell means from within my separation from others. No one else can make this decision for me, not the others in question or some outsider; no other circumstances may work any better. By emphasizing the necessity of a personal decision here, Cavell may make it seem as if seeing others as humans is merely subjective or whimsical, like deciding to order fish for dinner or to wear a yellow shirt instead of a blue one, or that it is inordinately difficult, like deciding to move or change jobs. We need once more to recall, however, the astonishing fact of the extent to which we *do* agree in judgment—astonishing because our mutual attunement is "unsponsored" by anything outside our own decisions. We determine the humanity of others on the basis of empathic projection—nothing more, but nothing less. Anything more than empathic projection (nature, say) would impinge on our responsibility; anything less (whim, say, or accident) would fail to account for the depth of our mutual attunement. "Empathic projection" here is not so much a technical term or solution as a name for the complex process whereby we recognize in others a humanness identical to what we understand our own humanity to be.

In deciding that some others are human, then, we are at the same time declaring our capacity to read them as

well as admitting their capacity to read us according to criteria that we (as humans) share. Our problem in practice is
not determining whether X is a human or whether those
lines on a face signify a scowl but dealing with what we
know—avoiding or acknowledging it, Cavell would say.
Our everyday statements to one another are accordingly
not more-or-less probable reports about one another but
responses to what we already know. "I know you are in
pain" does not simply impart information but extends sympathy. And "you are a human being" is not just a fact but
my fate for you, my response to your claim on me (CR, 428).
When I avoid others, knowledge does not fail me; like the
slave owner, I try not to face what I know. Acknowledgment
of others, on the other hand, goes beyond knowledge not
by uncovering new information but by acting on what we
know.

The other-minds skeptic construes our distance from
others in terms of ignorance, making our metaphysical finitude—our separation from others—an insoluble intellectual
lack or problem (we cannot know them). While also insisting on our separateness, Cavell, by contrast, pictures it
in terms of avoidance and acknowledgment, terms that
insist on our responsibility to one another, our role in what
joins or parts us. The skeptic, Cavell notes, scoops mind
out of behavior, leaving the body not so much hollow as
inanimate, neither hiding nor expressing anything. (The
crucified human body, he says at one point adapting Wittgenstein, is the best picture of the unacknowledged human
soul [CR, 430].) Cavell, by contrast, emphasizes the body's
expressiveness, which is not to say "that the man impaled
upon his sensation must express it in his behavior; it is to
say that in order not to express it he must *suppress* the behavior, or twist it. And if he twists it far or often enough, he
may lose possession of the region of the mind which that
behavior is expressing" (MWM, 264). Our "condemnation
to meaning" results from our being "separate creatures of
sense and soul," for whom "meaning is a matter of expression; and . . . expressionlessness is not a reprieve from
meaning, but a particular mode of it; and . . . the arrival of
an understanding is a question of acknowledgment" (WV,

107). (A living human body is the best picture of the ac-knowledged human soul.)

DECONSTRUCTION AND OTHER-MINDS SKEPTICISM

Other-minds skepticism in significant ways resembles the arguments in literary theory that I reviewed earlier. In deal-ing with others, the deconstructive literary theorist, like the other-minds skeptic, feels limited to merely indirect, arbitrary signs (for Miller this means that we "can never con-front the other person as an immediate presence, only en-counter indirect signs and traces of his passage"[23]); both suspect that our criteria for interpreting these signs are dis-appointingly provisional or local, maybe good enough for most practical purposes but lacking firmer ground (as de Man puts it, "our entire social system of language is an in-tricate system of rhetorical devices" [BI, 9], or "conventions of duplicity and dissimulation," masking "the inherent vio-lence of the actual relationships between human beings" [BI, 215–16]); and both leave other people ineluctably hid-den behind unreadable signifiers, blank looks, and dense barriers, if there at all. For the literary theorist, the other turns out to be unintelligible, inanimate, empty, like the shell analyzed by Miller in his reading of *The Prelude*. "No one is there for anyone," Derrida concludes, "not even for himself" (OG, 233). No one can be.

Everything said about people by the deconstructive theo-rist also applies to poems. As I have suggested, in critics as different as Coleridge, Krieger, and Poulet, either poetry benefits from the intelligibility of others, becoming one way among many of making ourselves known, or poetry secures the intelligibility of others, becoming the only way of dis-covering ourselves or making ourselves known, that is, the only way of surmounting the duplicity and evasiveness that riddle other uses of language. From the point of view of the reader, poems for these critics resemble especially open, honest, lucid people who let us look deep inside themselves, as Poulet suggests. From the point of view of the writer, poems allow for authentic self-discovery and self-expression. In different ways, Miller, de Man, and Derrida infect poetry with the indirectness, disingenuousness, and pretense that obtain elsewhere, leaving the self ostensibly disclosed or found in poetry as inauthentic and ill-formed as the self that we meet or put on everyday. Instead of humanizing poems, deconstructive critics thus textualize people and go on to question all efforts at deciphering others. Poulet describes reading in sexual terms—the poem letting the reader look deep inside itself with unheard of license, yielding "with little resistance to the importunities of the mind," and docilely allowing the reader to say farewell and thus avoid "the encumbrances of too prolonged a life in common." Miller and Derrida, by contrast, represent sex in textual terms, lovemaking being for them one way among many of discovering the inaccessibility of others and the omnipresence of language that keeps us disconnected. We are left with what de Man calls "the total impossibility of any contact, of any human communication, even in the most disinterested love."[24]

Associating recent theory with other-minds skepticism in this way allows me to characterize one of its moods. Like the other-minds skeptic, the literary theorists that I have mentioned profess disappointment in our opportunities for knowing one another. These opportunities, including poetry, seem too indirect (they fail to secure our immediate presence to one another) and too arbitrary (they depend on our abiding by merely local criteria, deciding to count that as a smile, that as irony, and so on), which is a way of saying that these so-called opportunities exacerbate the separateness that we think they overcome. As in external-world skepticism, separateness feels like an insoluble problem, almost a curse or punishment. Miller accordingly uses Stevens to speak of "a perpetual distance, desire, dissatisfaction, an 'emptiness that would be filled'" (LM, 418) and Derrida uses Rousseau to note "the anguish of dispersion" (OG, 277).

Forced to choose between the disappointment felt by the deconstructionists and the satisfaction in poetry expressed by the New Critics and Poulet, Cavell, I think, would take the former. Disappointment does greater justice to our distance from one another, to the feeling that a work of genius may, in fact often does, want its appropriate form and that (Poulet and Barzun notwithstanding) works of literature, like people, do not automatically open themselves up to us. Disappointment responds to the fact that I must decide on the validity of my reading from within my present condition: no one else can do it for me, or spare me of the effort and responsibility that having to decide entails.

But if the optimism of a Poulet borders on complacency, the disappointment of the deconstructionists similarly makes things too easy for us. For Miller, de Man, and Derrida, epistemological assumptions keep freeing us from ethical dilemmas: from being there for another, from acknowledging someone's pain or evading it, from hiding violence or expressing it, from giving in to desire or repressing it, from overcoming shame or succumbing to it. Because we cannot know others, we are relieved of the responsibility to read them accurately or face them. Because we are ineluctably hidden, we are not answerable for hiding.

Relieving us from responsibility may be one consequence of recent theory but its motives are more complex. Again, the deconstructionist's disappointment is presumably fueled by a demand for certainty, or at least directness, in communication. Longing really to know others, the deconstructionist is dissatisfied with the mendacity of literature, its being on a par with everything else that claims to fill the emptiness between us and others but finally cannot. Let down even by literature, not to mention lovemaking and ordinary language, the deconstructionist laments the irredeemable anguish of dispersion that results.

Cavell's account of other-minds skepticism encourages us to look beneath the disappointment I have described and to see the deconstructionist as not so much discovering his distance from others as trying—unsuccessfully—to distance himself from them. Instead of being ineluctably hemmed in by language, for Cavell our relationships with others are exposed—to our confusion, our hesitation, our courage, our fear, to everything that makes up our history. (What I have variously called in this chapter our intimacy or mutual attunement is another way of picturing our constant exposure to others, our legibility.) From this point of view, our condemnation to meaning tempts the deconstructionist to look for a reprieve that he finally cannot get, or can only get by trying to empty the text, even kill it. Instead of justifying the deconstructionist's actions, the quest for certain knowledge of the text excuses them. What looks like doubt brought on by the insistence on well-grounded insight into the text ends up resembling avoidance of what the text and language disclose. The deconstructionist's violence against the text is not the unintended consequence of his longing for a surer connection with it, as the deconstructionist himself would have it. The presence of the text is for some reason the deconstructionist's problem, not its absence. He wants the hollowed-out, indecipherable text that he gets.

Instead of satisfying the demand of the other-minds skeptic for certainty—say by furnishing more information about others—Cavell derives it from a desire to evade what the other-minds skeptic already knows. As the slave owner example suggests, "the alternative to my acknowledgment of the other is not my ignorance of him"—an ignorance to be answered with knowledge—"but my avoidance of him, call it my denial of him" (CR, 389)—a denial exposed by my everyday attitude toward the other. I have begun in this chapter to take a comparable view of deconstruction, using its similarities to other-minds skepticism to shed light on what other critics see as its gratuitous, or misguided, preoccupation with certainty. Intimacy, not dispersion, unsettles the deconstructionist—or so the analogy with other-minds skepticism suggests.

I emphasize "suggests" here. In this chapter I have been connecting deconstruction and other-minds skepticism by looking at several statements made by Miller, de Man, and Derrida. To complete my analysis, I need to show other-minds skepticism at work in the deconstructionist's treatment of texts—his attitude toward them, as Cavell would say. Cavell makes a similar move when (in *Must We Mean What We Say?* and in *The Claim of Reason*) he completes his account of other-minds skepticism by considering tragedy: *King Lear* in *Must We Mean What We Say?* and three other Shakespearean tragedies in *The Claim of Reason*. He takes

up tragedy because "both skepticism and tragedy conclude
with the condition of human separation, with a discovering that I am I. . . . Acknowledgment is to be studied, is
what is studied, in the avoidances that tragedy studies"
(CR, 389). In addition to exemplifying other-minds skepticism, tragedy shows its considerable power. As I show in
my next chapter, the avoidances that tragedy studies (for
example, in Othello's interrogating and finally smothering
Desdemona) reappear in de Man and Derrida's handling of
texts.

4

SKEPTICISM, TRAGEDY, AND THE COMEDY OF REMARRIAGE

CAVELL'S DISCUSSION OF other-minds skepticism, as I have presented it in my last chapter, suggests that at some level we cannot doubt that someone else is a human being. Although like the slave owner we can try to avoid this knowledge, our very efforts expose what we want to hide. Our turning from others—and not, say, simply being uncertain about them—points to something in us (shame, for example, or embarrassment) and not to something missing in them (a soul or a sound mind or body). Although empathic projection at first seems so fragile or disappointing a basis for knowing others, it turns out to be so strong that we have to act on it in one way or another. For Cavell, there are some things we cannot just not know: someone else's humanity is one of them.[1]

My rendition of Cavell's thinking on these matters raises several issues, some of which I will be addressing in this chapter. Drawing on his discussion of tragedy, I want to show what forms avoidance can take and how Cavell can presume to spot it. Then, using Cavell's account of the comedy of remarriage, I explore what acknowledgment looks like, or requires, as well as what it means to be touched by other-minds skepticism but not maimed by it. Finally, I extend to literary experience what Cavell says about acknowledging, avoiding, and reading people. The unlikely examples of Othello and Clark Gable help explain why certainty is the necessarily frustrated aim of de Man and Derrida, the goal they love to miss.

I want to emphasize that in turning to Shakespeare and to film, Cavell is not simply documenting ideas already gleaned from philosophy. (Cavell's treatment of Romantic literature—for him still another source of insight into skepticism—will be the subject of my next chapter.) If anything,

for him philosophical expressions of skepticism "intellectu-
alize" problems first worked out in literature.[2] By "intellec-
tualize" Cavell means that what philosophy presents as
doubt brought on by the (necessarily unsuccessful) quest for
certain knowledge, literature interprets as tragedy and even
murder, precipitated by an individual's need to deny something. In tragedy, skepticism results "not from a disappointment over a failure of knowledge"—as the skeptic himself
would have it—"but from a disappointment over its success
(even, from a horror of its success)" (CR, 476), a horror that
in Lear and Othello turns out to be deadly.

<h2 style="text-align:center">THE AVOIDANCE OF LOVE IN
KING LEAR AND *OTHELLO*</h2>

Cavell's reading of *King Lear* (published in *Must We Mean
What We Say?*) finds avoidance just about everywhere in the
play—in Lear's avoiding being recognized by Gloucester,
even testing Gloucester's eyes to make sure they are gone
before revealing himself (IV.vi.141–51, 172–74); Cornwall's
blinding Gloucester to avoid being seen by him; Gloucester's
failing to acknowledge Edmund as his son, "with *his* [Ed-
mund's] feelings of illegitimacy and being cast out" (MWM,
276); Edgar's avoiding being recognized by his father when
he comes upon him in act IV; and Lear's disavowing his love
for Cordelia, first by asking her to dissimulate love in the
abdication scene (something her sisters are quite ready—
and able—to do) and finally by wanting at the end of the
play to go off with her to prison, where their love can hide.
Several overlapping feelings motivate avoidance in the play,
among them guilt in the case of Cornwall (his putting out
Gloucester's eyes expresses the need of cruelty not to be
seen), shame in Gloucester (Gloucester withholds recognition of Edmund lest he be recognized as the father of a
bastard), fear as well as shame in Lear's attitude toward
Cordelia—more exactly, fear of love, love having presented
itself to Lear as a demand that he thinks he is, or may be,
unable to meet and as a need that makes him feel weak,
even helpless.

Cavell emphasizes the familiarity of these evasions, again

showing that in human relationships we are exposed to the worst as well as the best possibilities not just once (for instance, in war or love) but all the time. Edgar, for example, hesitates before revealing himself to his father in act IV in part because instead of seeing his father maimed and impotent, "he wants his father still to be a father, powerful, so that *he* can remain a child." "For otherwise," Cavell continues, "they are simply two human beings in need of one another, and it is not usual for parents and children to manage that transformation, becoming for one another nothing more, but nothing less, than unaccommodated men" (MWM, 285). In wanting Cordelia at once to proclaim her love for him and betray it, Lear similarly shows "the ordinariness of the scene, its verisimilitude to common parental love, swinging between absorption and rejection of its offspring, between encouragement to a rebellion they failed to make, and punishment for it" (MWM, 291).[3]

The ordinariness of Lear's actions needs emphasizing not only because he is a king but because his feelings for Cordelia may seem unusual, even incestuous, and hence uniquely conducive to guilt and shame. While agreeing that Lear's relationship with Cordelia is incompatible with her having any other lover, Cavell suggests (rightly, I think) that avoidance of love and avoidance of a particular kind of love interpret one another in this play:

> Avoidance of love is always, or always begins as, an avoidance of a particular kind of love: men do not just naturally not love, they learn not to. . . . And the avoidance of a particular love, or the acceptance of it, will spread to every other; every love, in acceptance or rejection, is mirrored in every other. It is part of the miracle of the vision in *King Lear* to bring this before us, so that we do not care whether the *kind* of love felt between these two is forbidden according to man's lights. We care whether love is or is not altogether forbidden to man, whether we may not altogether be incapable of it, of admitting it into our world. (MWM, 300)

We can generalize from Lear's actions not despite the particularity of his love but because of it. Avoidance, like acknowledgment, is always specific, inspired by a feeling or incident determinate enough to require a response. I can safely admit that some parents mistreat their children; my own actions (because they are specific and thus mine, or me) are harder to face—and therefore more tempting to avoid.[4]

In keeping with the point that tragedy results not from the failure of knowledge but from horror of its success, Cavell claims that knowledge does not fail the characters in *King Lear*. Lear knows that at the outset of the play he is offering Cordelia a bribe, asking her to make him only look like a loved man, thus concealing their genuine intimacy ("She is his joy," Cavell notes; "she knows it and he knows it" [MWM, 290]). Lear's problem is not uncertainty, to be answered by proof of Cordelia's love or disloyalty. His problem is accepting what he already knows, a problem to be solved—but how? Not by Cordelia, at least not in the opening scene, where her silence does not so much compel Lear to acknowledge their intimacy as keep alive the possibility of his one day facing it—a possibility that terrifies him.

Avoidance—disguised as a request for knowledge—thus motivates Lear's otherwise bizarre actions in the opening scene. ("Tell me," Lear says to his daughters, "Which of you shall we say doth love us most," as if he did not know.) Only avoidance can explain some of the other extraordinary scenes in the play, such as Edgar's leading Gloucester up a nonexistent hill to an imaginary cliff for an obviously doomed-in-advance attempt at suicide. The scene is grotesque, as critics since Wilson Knight have felt; it does not make any sense or, rather, for Cavell it only makes sense as a grotesquely literal "consequence of avoiding the facts": "It is not the emblem of the Lear universe, but an instance of what has led its minds to their present state: there are no lengths to which we may not go in order to avoid being revealed, even to those we love and are loved by. Or rather, especially to those we love and are loved by: to other people it is *easy* not to be known" (MWM, 284). In default of any better explanation, Edgar and Gloucester's dialogue illustrates "what people will *have* to say and try to mean to one another when they are incapable of acknowledging to one another what they have to acknowledge" (MWM, 284).

In italicizing "have" here, Cavell calls attention to the kind of necessity at work in this play, a necessity resulting not from fate or divine justice but from the logic of avoidance. Although these characters' evasions seem contingent, predicated in Lear's case on a seemingly unnecessary terror of being loved, nobody knows what might have prevented them. Blaming Lear accordingly seems inappropriate not because he is faultless but because we cannot imagine any position from which we can correct him. On one level Lear's bribing his daughters is his choice; on another it logically, even inevitably, follows from his fear, a fear so deeply lodged in his character as to make anything we would say or do in response feel trite.

Lear's attempts at avoidance fail; he is caught, exposed, found out, to use some of the phrases I introduced in my last chapter. Trying to conceal his love of Cordelia kills her as well as him. The thwarting of his plans and Cornwall's need to avoid being seen by Gloucester are for Cavell fragile signs of hope—hope not that we can, or will, do better than these characters but that "*every* falsehood, every refusal of acknowledgment will be tracked down" (MWM, 309), if not in the world, then at least in what Cavell calls, following Kierkegaard, the realm of the spirit. This hope for spiritual justice, however, is obviously purchased at an extreme price—the death of Lear and Cordelia. Lear is unable to acknowledge his love but also unable to hide it (and thereby avoid the world) or to get rid of it (and thereby avoid love). Although his loving Cordelia makes him heroic and sets him off from the mercenaries surrounding him, his inability to acknowledge his love—rather, his acknowledging his love only by trying to avoid it, as if it were shameful—makes him tragic. Death does not so much solve his problem as eliminate it, pointing up its insolubility.

In *Lear*, as in the slave owner example mentioned in my last chapter, knowledge—here, Lear's knowing that he loves Cordelia—does not substitute for acknowledgment. Whatever its value as a reading of *King Lear*, the relevance of this conclusion to skepticism is initially hard to fathom. As if aware of the apparent unlikelihood of a connection between Lear's tragedy and skepticism, Cavell makes the historical point that replacing acknowledgment with knowledge in the (vain) hope that we can save our lives only by knowing them is also one legacy of modern epistemology, which begins in the writings of Galileo, Bacon, and Descartes, Shakespeare's contemporaries. These thinkers start to define knowledge in terms of certainty and sense experience, suggesting that all genuine connection with the world hinges on what is present to the senses—and that turns out, Cavell says, "not to be the world" (MWM, 323). The world, in other words, "vanishes exactly with the effort [of these philosophers] to *make* it present" (MWM, 323)—much as Cordelia's love of Lear vanishes or at least fails to appear with Lear's apparent effort to determine publicly which of his daughters loves him. I say "apparent effort" because Cavell argues that Lear knows the answer to his own question: he asks the question not to flush his intimacy with Cordelia out into the open but to avoid it, even to prevent its ever appearing. If the epistemologist resembles Lear, then the epistemologist's demand for certain knowledge may similarly be disingenuous. His longing for the world's presence—his very need to make the world appear—may conceal avoidance of the world he already knows. Despite his professed wish to connect himself securely to the world, the epistemologist may want the vanishing of the world that he gets.

This interpretation of skepticism along the lines of Shakespearean tragedy is reinforced by Cavell's reading of Othello, who illustrates for Cavell "the murderous lengths to which narcissism [defined here as "a kind of denial of an existence shared with others"] must go in order to maintain its picture of itself as skepticism, in order to maintain its stand of ignorance, its fear or avoidance of knowing, under the color of a claim to certainty" (TS, 61). Cavell's reading of *Othello*, which concludes *The Claim of Reason*, is remarkably compressed, each sentence uncovering an often overlooked or minimized nuance of the play and relating it to the problem of knowledge that the play explores. Instead of reviewing this reading in all its detail, I will concentrate on the crucial sentence just quoted.

By Othello's "stand of ignorance," Cavell in part means Othello's professed uncertainty about Desdemona's virtue, his suspicion that she is a whore. "A claim to certainty" presumably fuels Othello's doubt: he wants to be absolutely sure that Desdemona is chaste—like the epistemologist, he will have "ocular proof." When the evidence (the handkerchief, for instance) apparently suggests Desdemona's guilt, or at least fails to demonstrate her innocence, Othello accordingly convicts her in the play's final scene.

I say "professed uncertainty" because in Cavell's view Othello in fact knows that Desdemona is innocent but tries to avoid that knowledge. Ignorance (of Desdemona's fidelity) is a stand he wants, maybe even has, to take; similarly, his commitment to certainty, instead of justifying or motivating his actions, belatedly tries to excuse them. In the terms of the play, although Othello knows the falsity of Iago's suspicions, he has a use for them. In Cavell's words, "however far he believes Iago's tidings, he cannot just believe them; somewhere he also *knows* them to be false" (CR, 488).

But where? How does Cavell know this? As with the slave owner and Lear, Othello's own actions betray him. His urgent latching on to Iago's version of things smacks of desperation, not dispassionate inquiry. Cavell derives this desperation not from Othello's failure with Desdemona (his impotence, say, or her frigidity) but from his success, his eliciting her desire. He is surprised that she is flesh and blood, the one thing this romantic hero does not want to see about himself (for if she is flesh and blood, then he must be, since they are one). In Cavell's words, "he cannot forgive Desdemona for existing, for being separate from him, outside, beyond command" (CR, 491), for contesting his pure image of himself, for making him face his own sexuality and mortality. His anxiously arrived at doubts about her faithfulness thus cover or evade what he experiences as an even more terrible certainty: Desdemona exists, is flesh and blood, separate, and in need. So is he.

Instead of confronting his own humanity, Othello thus tries to change the subject. He would rather make Desdemona's love "an intellectual difficulty, a riddle" (CR, 493), than acknowledge what it says about him. In tragedy we are forced to confront the consequences of our evasions. Othello's failure to acknowledge Desdemona not only denies her but turns his own heart to stone, illustrating what Cavell calls the "necessary reflexiveness of spiritual torture" (CR, 493). What Othello lacked was not knowledge, no matter how hard he tried to maintain his stand of ignorance or how often he pledged his allegiance to certainty. "He knew everything but he could not yield to what he knew, be commanded by it. He found out too much for his mind, not too little" (CR, 496).

Othello's tragedy, like Lear's, puts the skeptic's demand for certainty in a new light. Although apparently a sign of intellectual scrupulousness, this commitment to proof in Othello's case is motivated by a self-consuming disappointment in his mortality, which his relationship with Desdemona has revealed. Instead of facing what he knows, Othello would rather deny, or question, the intimacy that has made him so certain of his separateness. His "doubt" turns out to be fatal to himself as well as to Desdemona: it leads him to kill her, his world- and self-consuming revenge. If we let Othello's call for ocular proof interpret the skeptic's comparable longing for certainty, then what looks like doubt in skepticism brought on by the insistence on certainty may similarly be murder inspired by the need to deny or conceal something. In the guise of connecting himself more certainly to the world—and necessarily failing—the skeptic may be evading an uncomfortable connection already made.

Affirming Separateness: Skepticism and the Comedy of Remarriage

In discussing Cavell's treatment of *King Lear* and *Othello*, I have been trying to show how Cavell depicts avoidance and where he finds it. I turn now to consider what acknowledgment and living with skepticism amount to. I am, in effect, moving from tragedy to comedy and, more specifically, to the comedies of remarriage examined in *Pursuits of Happiness*. Cavell suggests that happiness, maybe even sanity, depends on being touched by Othello's problems but not done in by them (CR, 453). *Pursuits of Happiness* follows several couples in search of this difficult goal.

The Lady Eve, It Happened One Night, Bringing up Baby, The

Philadelphia Story, His Girl Friday, Adam's Rib, and *The Awful Truth* make up the genre that Cavell calls the comedy of remarriage. Among the several features of this genre discussed in *Pursuits of Happiness,* the following bear especially on tragedy and the problem of other minds:

1. Each of these films traces a struggle between a man and a woman, a struggle for what Cavell variously calls equality, mutual freedom, and reciprocal acknowledgment.

2. Conversations between the hero and heroine contribute to their acknowledging one another, more specifically to their forgiving one another and thus forgoing their understandable disappointment in one another and consequent desire for revenge.

3. Before acknowledging one another, both the man and the woman must change—the man by relinquishing his control of himself and the relationship (often by making a fool of himself, for example, by singing) and the woman by resurrecting, or finally expressing, her desire.

4. The threat, sometimes even the fact, of divorce and separation in these films suggests that these individuals' personal willingness for remarriage—not the church, the state, or even children—authenticates their relationship. Although the state cannot keep the couple together, it nevertheless can allow them to find one another or find within the world enough space and time for being together. (The world can get out of their way.) Marriage takes on national importance not because the state sanctions these marriages but because these marriages legitimize the state as a place where personal happiness can still be sought and found.[5]

5. These characters make room for their relationship not once and for all (in a wedding ceremony, say) but every day. Their lives are held together not by an event but by their attitude toward events—their capacity for adventure, improvisation, and sociability. In *The World Viewed* Cavell finds improvisation in the very grain of film, where "however studied the lines and set the business, the movement of the actors [is] essentially improvised—as in those everyday actions in which we walk through a new room or lift a cup in an unfamiliar locale or cross a street or greet a friend or look in a store window or accept an offered cigarette or add a

thought to a conversation. They could all go one way or another" (WV, 153). He defines sociability in the following recollection of his own father in conversation with strangers, putting them at ease, in a shop, a lobby, a train, "animated, laughing, comparing notes": "He knew no more about the other than the other knew about him. He seemed merely able to act on what nobody could fail to know, and to provide what nobody could fail to appreciate, even if in a given moment they could not return it. Call it sociability" (TS, 105).

These couples' lives together thus remain "unsponsored," the courage and imagination required for their happiness being qualities that a ceremony can neither reward nor ensure (PH, 239). "Unsponsored" is a favorite word of Cavell's for describing these relationships—he uses it again, for example, in *The World Viewed*, when he writes "If all modern love is perverse, because now tangential to the circling of society, then the promise of love depends upon the acceptance of perversity, and that in turn requires the strength to share privacy, to cohabit in one element, unsponsored by society" (WV, 67). I hear in the word the final lines of Wallace Stevens's "Sunday Morning," which also speaks of our living in an "old dependency of day and night, / Or island solitude, unsponsored, free." In referring to modern love, Cavell is suggesting that we live in a new dependency of day and night that derives in part from our loss of faith in the ability of society to provide the continuity affirmed by classical comedy. Modern romance shows not only that one couple can make it alone, unsponsored, but that they have to make it on their own. Their happiness cannot wait or count on the support of their culture but depends on personal qualities such as "wit, invention [cf. improvisation], good spirits, the capacity to entertain [cf. sociability], and the grace to retain oneself, since these are no longer had for the hiring" (WV, 79).

The picture emerging from these films (Cavell is commenting specifically on *It Happened One Night*) is that the existence of others is something that we know but can try to repress. As in *Lear* and *Othello*, this repression, or avoidance, "does violence to others, it separates their bodies from their souls, makes monsters of them; and presumably we do it because we feel that others are doing this violence to us" (PH, 109). "The release from this circle of vengeance" (PH, 109), Cavell continues, is acknowledgment. Again there is no substituting knowledge for acknowledgment, no transcending the barrier between others and us without acting: "you have to act in order to make things happen, night and day; and to act from within the world, within your connection with others, forgoing the wish for a place outside from which to view and to direct your fate. These are at best merely further fates. There is no place to go in order to acquire the authority of connection" (PH, 109). As discussed in chapter 3, I must act on internal grounds, from within my empathic projection of humanity onto another, not just once and for all (at a wedding, say) but every day. There is no better time or place than here and now to acknowledge someone else.

This account of the comedy of remarriage may make it seem radically opposed to Shakespearean tragedy, with comedy celebrating, or at least accepting, everything that tragedy is uneasy with: acknowledgment (as opposed to avoidance); forgiveness (versus disappointment and revenge); change, repetition, and everyday life (versus Lear's desire to solve the problem of love by swapping, once and for all, his fortune for false love, or Othello's vow that "to be once in doubt / Is once to be resolved"); sociability and love (not isolation); putting together body and soul, perception and imagination (instead of violently pulling them apart, thereby turning bodies into monsters, corpses, or statues and allowing imagination to stoke suspicion and fear rather than desire). Despite these differences, the two genres overlap and even feed into one another. As Cavell explains in "The Avoidance of Love," "comedy is fun because it can purge us of the unnatural and of the merely natural by laughing at us and singing to us and dancing for us, and by making us laugh and sing and dance. The tragedy is that comedy has its limits. This is part of the sadness within comedy; the emptiness after a long laugh. Join hands here as we may, one of the hands is mine and the other is yours" (MWM, 339–40).[6]

Farce and melodrama show the permeability of the boundary separating tragedy from comedy. Cavell uses *Othello* to illustrate how tragedy borders on farce and thus approaches comedy. The staples of farce keep appearing in the play—in its precipitous rhythm, its beginning with an offstage sexual scene, and its questioning the relationship between marriage and romance, not to mention its hero's declared uncertainty about his wife's chastity and its heroine's bawdy wit. The play, however, smothers the laughter that these elements of farce might have triggered. In another context another man might have delighted in Desdemona's capacity for pleasure. Othello uses it against her.

Why Othello uses it against her is as difficult to understand, let alone remedy, as the fear and disappointment that motivate him. Cavell's discussion of tragedy ends not with a simple prescription for avoiding tragedy but with a complex question: "How do we stop? How do we learn that what we need is not more knowledge," as Lear and Othello's requests for information and proof would suggest, "but the willingness to forgo knowing?" (MWM, 324)—that is, to forgo asking questions that dodge what we already know. Putting the problem this way underscores its enormity. Little wonder Cordelia's sense of what Lear is doing renders her speechless, as if stunned. "What shall Cordelia speak?" Her dilemma is ours, or the predicament of anyone touched by Lear's needs in this scene. Acknowledgment is not a magic wand forever releasing us from revenge, fear, and so on but an arduous task.

The ambiguous endings of *The Philadelphia Story* and the other comedies of remarriage respect the fragility of comedy, or, what is the same thing, the tremendous obstacles in comedy's way. *The Philadelphia Story* ends not with an embrace signifying happiness but with a photograph of an embrace, "something at a remove from what has gone before, hence betokening uncertainty" (PH, 160). The equivocal conclusions of these films fit the open-endedness of the relationships they study, that is, the dependency of these relationships on improvisation and on these couples' willingness to remarry not just once but every day. The conversations that animate these marriages can always break off or turn into the ironic, sadistic exchanges that Cavell finds in a melodrama like *Gaslight*. These latter exchanges aim at stupefying and finally silencing the woman instead of recreating her.[7] (Just as tragedy abuts farce and thus approaches comedy, comedy borders on melodrama and thus approaches tragedy.)

The entanglement of comedy and tragedy constantly puts the characters in these remarriage comedies between acknowledgment and avoidance and between forgiveness and revenge. Put differently, although irony is never inevitable (as it is in de Man), it is always an option for the participants in these films' conversations.[8] The laughter in these films is finally more good-humored and therapeutic than rueful, but bitterness is always a possibility.

A crucial scene in *It Happened One Night* highlights the vulnerability of the happiness achieved in these comedies. Clark Gable, separated from Claudette Colbert by a makeshift curtain in their auto camp cabin, dreams out loud of his ideal girl while Colbert prepares for bed:

> If I ever met the right sort of girl, I'd—. Yeah, but where are you going to find her, somebody that's real, somebody that's alive? They don't come that way any more. I've even been sucker enough to make plans. I saw an island in the Pacific once. Never been able to forget it. That's where I'd like to take her. But she'd have to be the sort of girl that'd jump in the surf with me and love it as much as I did. You know, those nights when you and the moon and the water all become one and you feel that you're part of something big and marvelous. Those are the only places to live. Where the stars are so close over your head that you feel you could reach right up and stir them around. Certainly I've been thinking about it. Boy, if I could ever find a girl who's hungry for those things. (Quoted in PH, 97)

Although Cavell does not make this point, I hear in Gable's speech the kind of imagination that won over another young woman, Desdemona. Like Desdemona, Colbert acts; she comes around the blanket/curtain, approaches his bedside, throws her arms around him, and declares her love for him.

Like Othello, Gable seems stunned, even speechless, not because his words have failed but because they have worked all too well. After Colbert retreats to her own bed, apologizing and sobbing, Gable asks, "Hey, Brat. Did you mean that? Would you really go [with me]?" But it is too late. She is asleep.

Gable's balking, his failure to see his dream in Colbert's reality, his being surprised by her flesh-and-blood existence, even threatened by it, and his belatedly excusing his own fears as uncertainty (did she really mean it? can I be sure?)—all of these show his kinship with Othello. Cavell refuses to minimize Gable's failure here: it is "never fully compensated for," but "remains an eye of pain, a source of suspicion and compromise haunting the happy end of this drama" (PH, 101), like the photographs that conclude *The Philadelphia Story*. Gable's inaction marks the film's conclusion as unstable, open to change, and forever contingent on these characters' own actions. Nevertheless, the film ends happily, with his acknowledging that she's the right sort of girl—a girl, and thus subject to the same anxieties that have touched him, a man—but the right sort, the one he admits he needs. Instead of resenting her reality (her separateness), he is hungry for it, much as Colbert's finally accepting food from Gable allows her to admit her own need for him.[9]

I said in my last chapter that the epistemology of deconstruction makes things too easy for us by releasing us from ethical dilemmas. Gable's faltering acceptance of Colbert clarifies this point. As he dreams out loud of the right sort of girl, his voice, Cavell notes, "penetrate[s] [Colbert] as she follows it; her body expands with the imagination of what he is envisioning; her head arches back as her eyes close" (PH, 98). The power of his voice here, along with the importance of conversation to all these films, recalls Derrida's comment on speech supposedly "[penetrating] into me violently, it is the privileged route for forced entry and interiorization" (see above, pp. 53–54).

Derrida is restating a logocentric myth that he will go on to subvert by showing that the flesh-and-blood presence allegedly announced by a voice forever eludes us. The scene in *It Happened One Night* acquires its tension from everything that Derrida undermines here. Instead of helplessly yielding to a violent, intrusive force, Colbert is free to acknowledge or avoid the desire that Gable's speech touches. Gable similarly has to face or turn away from her all-too-real immediate presence before him. It would be easier for him if she were not by his bed, if, as Derrida suggests, she could not be (given the impossibility of direct presence). But she is. She means what she says when she declares her love for him, however much Gable may want to put her comments and her presence into question.

In interrogating the possibility of presence, or making presence an intellectual/linguistic problem, Derrida in effect sanctions Gable's own Othello-like attempt at uncertainty (his asking, after failing to take advantage of Colbert's overture, did you really mean it?). In much the same way, de Man's remarks on shame and language, also cited in my previous chapter, participate in Lear's own desire to avoid expressing his love. As de Man might put it, in the abdication scene Lear is looking for words from Cordelia to hide behind, an expression from her that will not coincide with what nevertheless in this play has to be expressed, namely, their love for one another. It would be easier for Lear if sign and meaning could never coincide, if he could hide meaning behind a misleading sign or find a rhetorical device that would allow him to escape from expressing his unnameable desires. But Lear cannot do these things, though tragically he tries.

ACKNOWLEDGMENT AND AVOIDANCE IN LITERARY THEORY

So far I have been discussing how avoidance and acknowledgment figure in human relationships, as studied by Cavell in tragedy and the comedies of remarriage. I want finally to consider how these same terms also apply to our relationships as readers with literary texts. Following Cavell, I will be arguing, first, that there are some things about texts that we cannot just not know but must work at avoiding, ignoring, or repressing and, secondly, that such willed uncertainty marks the theorizing of de Man and Derrida.

Cavell's fullest discussion of acknowledgment and avoidance in literary criticism occurs appropriately enough in the *King Lear* essay.[10] Commenting on his reading of the play, Cavell notes that he has responded to such traditional cruxes as Lear's motivation in the opening scene, Gloucester's blinding, and Edgar's delay before revealing himself to his father, to name only a few. He has addressed these problems because of their familiarity, not despite it. He has approached them, moreover, by "sticking as continuously to the text as [he] can—that is, avoiding theorizing about the data [he can] provide for [his] assertions, appealing to any considerations which, in conscience, convince [him] of their correctness" (MWM, 272).

Cavell's account of his procedure raises several questions. What considerations or data support a reading? Why should he stop, or not start, theorizing?[11] How does theorizing relate to the cruxes in question? These questions reduce to one, put by Cavell this way: if what he says about *King Lear* is correct, why have other critics failed to see it? In Cavell's own words, "since whatever critical discoveries I can claim to have made hardly result from unheard of information, full conviction in them awaits a convincing account of what has kept them covered" (MWM, 272). For critics uneasy with talk of correctness, data, and sticking to the text, Cavell makes things worse instead of better when he goes on to claim not only obviousness but completeness for his reading. By "obvious," he does not mean "certain" but familiar, or something within everyone's view; by "complete," he does not mean "exhaustive" but thorough, or something that results from staying with the text and not fleeing it. Cavell needs to explain why, if his reading is so obvious, it has eluded previous critics. His problem here matches Wittgenstein's in the *Philosophical Investigations,* "where the aspects of things that are most important to us are hidden because of their simplicity and familiarity. (One is unable to notice something—because it is always before one's eyes.)" (no. 129). Wittgenstein's remark of course does not solve Cavell's problem but helps us formulate it more precisely. What is always before our eyes in *King Lear* and why do we shy away from it?

According to Cavell, *King Lear* itself explores the difficulty of seeing the obvious, presenting it as a refusal or failure to acknowledge something already known. Within the play the obvious is not there for people to see if they would only look, like a star overhead. Instead, the obvious is something seen but often shunned, as Edgar avoids his maimed father. As this last example suggests, our alleged failing as spectators or readers to notice the obvious in *King Lear* recalls the characters' evasions in the play and thus implicates us in their tragedy. Our missing something in the play, like Lear trying not to acknowledge something in his relationship with Cordelia, reflects not our ignorance but our own "refusal to see," our "willful, complicitous" neglect of what is presumably in front of us (MWM, 313).

Cavell is suggesting that as critics we have not been ignorant of the obvious considerations that support his reading; instead, we have avoided them. As Cavell realizes, avoiding a play presupposes our being able to acknowledge it. Before specifying how we acknowledge these characters' lives, Cavell rules out the possibility of our directly intervening in them, say by rushing on stage to save Desdemona or warning Othello of Iago's treachery. These actions might occur to us if we encountered a man trying to hurt a woman in real life. Faced with a murder in progress outside the theater, we might blame ourselves for not intervening—for merely watching what was happening instead of getting involved. As Cavell puts it, only watching others outside the theater "shows a specific response to the claim they make upon us, a specific form of acknowledgment; for example, rejection" (MWM, 331) (in the case of a murder, rejection of the victim's claim on us, say her need for our help). Outside the theater, watching others can mean hiding from them or staying in the dark, staring at them from afar or closer up. By not making ourselves present to other people, we theatricalize them, turning their lives into a spectacle and their world into a stage that we (only) view.[12] The physical conditions of the theater thus highlight the hiddenness, isolation, inaction, and silence we can cultivate outside when we watch people instead of taking part in their lives. "Can" deserves to be emphasized here: whereas a theatrical(ized) society for Derrida is a tautology, for Cavell it is a costly choice.

This explanation of avoidance outside the theater poses difficult problems for acknowledgment inside the theater, where watching characters on stage seems not a culpable form of avoidance but an ordinary, even expected, response to a play. Nevertheless, despite this difference, Cavell insists that we acknowledge characters on stage much as we acknowledge people outside the theater, that is, "by revealing ourselves, by allowing ourselves to be seen" (MWM, 333). In a theater, however, "allowing ourselves to be seen" means not physically putting ourselves in the characters' presence (for example, by rushing on stage) but allowing the characters to be present to us. Allowing the characters to be present to us in turn means accepting our "separateness from what is happening to them; that I am I, and here. It is only in this perception of them as separate from me that I make them present. That I make them *other*, and face them" (MWM, 338). I cannot acknowledge their separateness without accepting my own; I cannot coherently declare that they are there without revealing that I am here.

Why then, Cavell concludes, do I do nothing in a theater when faced with tragic events?

> If I do nothing because I am distracted by the pleasures of witnessing this folly [on stage], or out of my knowledge of the proprieties of the place I am in [the theater, where sophisticated people do not jump on stage], or because I think there will be some more appropriate time in which to act [presumably when comparable events take place in real life], or because I feel helpless to un-do events of such proportion [even outside the theater I still watch tragedies, there being nothing else I can do], then I continue my sponsorship of evil in the world, its sway waiting upon these forms of inaction. I exit running [like Lear from his scene with the blinded Gloucester]. But if I do nothing because there is nothing to do, where that means that I have given over the time and space in which action is mine and consequently that I am in awe before the fact that I cannot do and suffer what it is another's to do and suf-

fer, then I confirm the final fact of our separateness. And that is the unity of our condition. (MWM, 339)

Outside the theater, when confronting tragic events, I call on numerous excuses to justify my inaction, my merely watching and not getting involved (I am distracted, I feel helpless, the time and place are not right, and so on). Inside the theater, avoidance takes the form of inattention or neglect rather than inaction. But declining to act and refusing to see both result from a wish for invisibility. Facing these characters, letting them be present, means facing my own separateness, something I can be as loathe to do as they are.

Seeing the obvious in a play—or allowing it to be present to you—thus entails allowing yourself to be seen. Not seeing the obvious or avoiding it results from not wishing to be seen.[13] Instead of further applying these points to Cavell's reading of *King Lear* and to Shakespeare criticism, I want to use these remarks to account for the avoidance I find in deconstruction.

Avoidance, as Cavell describes it, first shows up in the deconstructionist's often-noted insistence on certainty and theoretical rigor. The deconstructionist would have ocular proof: I say "ocular" not just to recall Othello but also to highlight the deconstructionist's need to see the text as a whole, to make all of it absolutely, simultaneously clear. The text in question is usually not strange but familiar, one with which the critic has been intimately acquainted. Familiarity with the text has not bred contempt but some kind of dissatisfaction, maybe boredom, if we listen to the many claims touting the excitement and pleasure afforded by recent theory.[14] The deconstructionist's efforts result not from a failure of knowledge or from ignorance, which might lead to historical research (among other possibilities), but from disappointment with what we already presumably know, which leads the deconstructionist to try to unsettle what seems obvious. Deconstructionists are concerned with an aspect of the text that they do not just not know but must work at unknowing.

Suspiciously interrogating the text and demanding to see all of it turn the text into an intellectual difficulty or riddle. The text vanishes with the effort to make it present, becoming a blank corpse, mysterious shell, indecipherable maze, or impenetrable stone, to use some of the metaphors brought up in my last chapter—hence the feeling that deconstructionists do violence to the text, even smother it with their theoretical concerns. In any case, the text dies or at least loses the intelligibility and life found in it by previous critics, sometimes even by deconstructionists in their earlier work. Othello's comment to Iago—"I think my wife be honest, and think she is not; / I think that thou art just, and think thou art not" (III.iii.384–85)—captures the bafflement of the deconstructive reader stymied by the text's aporias or antinomies.

Recalling the necessary reflexiveness of spiritual torture, I would suggest that the qualities removed from the text disappear from the deconstructionist's own writing, in de Man's case stripping it of personality, directness, concreteness, and at times even clarity: hence the starkness, the icy purity, of de Man's prose, its predilection for the passive voice, its penchant for abstractions and nominalizations, its tolerance for sweeping generalizations and impossible-to-track-down pronouns, its uneasiness with assertions of presence, and its delight in self-canceling paradoxes and ironies. Many readers have noticed these qualities in de Man's prose. One of the best recent treatments of his work, Stanley Corngold's "Error in Paul de Man," cites the "ungainly severity of the later style" as well as the "violence" of de Man's thought, "which adduces distinctions, disturbs their difference, and makes this abolition prove the void of indetermination," a void that sucks in and dissolves the self.[15] De Man does not so much exit running as refuse to appear in his prose, apparently not wishing to be seen.

Likening a theorist such as de Man to characters such as Lear and Othello suggests that this self-dissolution is not an unfortunate or inadvertent by-product of de Man's work but one of its underlying motives—despite de Man's declared obsession with really knowing a text, say by reading it more slowly or closely than other readers ordinarily do. Cavell notes that skepticism tends to "soberize, or respectify, or scientize itself, claiming, for example, greater precision or accuracy or intellectual scrupulousness than, for practical purposes, we are forced to practice in our ordinary lives" (IQO, 197). De Man's well-known concern for epistemological rigor—what one of his most sympathetic commentators calls his "almost obsessive preoccupation with truth"[16]—fits in with this tendency. As noted earlier, critics of deconstruction as otherwise different as E. D. Hirsch, Charles Altieri, and M. H. Abrams have taken this quest for rigor and certainty at face value, seeing it as laudable in science but misdirected and therefore bound to fail in literary criticism, where (these critics go on to add) we can nevertheless be probably sure, or sure enough, of our conclusions.[17] According to this critique, by insisting on certainty, deconstructionists (for some reason) bring on the doubts that befall them.

Cavell's interpretation of tragedy encourages us to take a different tack. De Man's doubts about what we know of a text, though on the surface motivated by what Abrams and others rightly call a misguided intellectual scrupulousness, derive from a (displaced) denial motivated by a self-consuming disappointment that seeks world-consuming revenge—a revenge leaving nothing outside the text (*il n'y a pas de hors-texte*, in Derrida's famous phrase). Staring hard at the text, though ostensibly meant to penetrate it, may thus distance the deconstructionist from it, much as staring at people may avoid a claim they make on us by rejecting it, or them. The deconstructionist may desire the unraveling of the text (really of all our efforts to make ourselves present) that he gets. Although this unraveling occurs at unsettling speed, it cannot happen soon, or often, enough.

Some reasons behind this wish not to be seen emerge in Cavell's account of Coriolanus, whose

> disgust with the world suggests that the skeptic's search for purity is not fundamental but motivated, that the repudiation of the world is not originally in response to the failure of intellectual certainty but before that a response to a vision of intellectual vulgarity, of commonness, call it a vision of communication as contamination, the discovery that human existence is

inherently undistinguished. . . . Coriolanus's disgust
is, as I read it, directly and emblematically a disgust
with language, with the vulgarity of the vulgar tongue.
(DK, 15)

I find such a recoil from vulgarity, such an experience of
"communication as contamination," in the several passages
from *Blindness and Insight* that I looked at in my last chapter,
especially in their claim that it is the distinctive "curse" of
everday language to hide meaning behind misleading signs.
(I should also mention Miller's reference to seemingly non-
verbal exchanges like lovemaking as being "contaminated by
language.") Disappointed by everyday life, with the apparent mendacity of the vulgar tongue, de Man takes revenge
on literature by debunking its pretensions to escape the inauthenticity that for him tarnishes ordinary talk. For human
existence to be universally undistinguished, literature (a
human product) has to partake of "the duplicity, the confusion, the untruth that we take for granted" in everything
else we do. The evasiveness of literary meaning thus follows not simply from a misapplied dedication to certainty—to be answered with evidence of what we can still claim
to know—but from the sordidness of our life together, what
de Man calls "the inherent violence of the actual relationships between human beings" (BI, 215–16). As a reader of
literary texts, de Man does not combat this violence but lets
it ramify. Nothing offsets this violence—not criticism, not
literature, not even love.

In drawing on Cavell's account of skepticism and tragedy,
I have been trying here not so much to answer de Man as to
indicate the level such a response must eventually explore,
that level being his deep disdain for human intercourse.
Like Lear's need to conceal his love for Cordelia, this disdain
is deeply rooted as well as difficult to remedy. More specifically, telling de Man that we can be sure enough about
meaning for most practical purposes sidesteps his dark vision of everyday linguistic practice—the vision that feeds
his desire to demystify literature. Experiencing communication as contamination, as implicating him in a human
community he wants to disavow, de Man's seemingly scru-

pulous questioning forestalls our ever communicating in literary as well as ordinary language.

IN CONCLUDING HIS ACCOUNT of traditional epistemology in *The Claim of Reason*, Cavell remarks that "to be interested in such accounts [of skepticism], as accounts of the cost of knowing to the knowing creature, I suppose one will have to take an interest in certain preoccupations of romanticism" (CR, 242). To complete the account of deconstruction I have begun here, I turn to these preoccupations in my next chapter.

5

STANLEY CAVELL'S
ROMANTICISM

CAVELL NOT ONLY WRITES about the Romantics but emulates them in analyzing both external-world and other-minds skepticism. He admires the Romantics, finding it "especially brave of Thoreau," for example, "to have recognized the achievement of sanity as the goal, or ratification, of his arrangements" (CR, 469) and applauding Blake's "brave acceptance of the sufficiency of human finitude, an achievement of the complete disappearance of its disappointment, in oneself and in others, an acknowledgment of satisfaction and of reciprocity" (CR, 471). By "the Romantics" here, I mean Emerson, Poe, and Thoreau as well as Blake, Wordsworth, and Coleridge. (Cavell has so far written very little about Shelley, Keats, and Byron.) In concluding my discussion of Cavell's response to skepticism, I will be glancing at his treatment of all these writers but I will be concentrating on *The Senses of Walden,* his book on Thoreau.

I choose this book in part because it most directly confronts some of the issues raised by recent literary theory. The Thoreau scholar William Howarth has even suggested that in *The Senses of Walden* Cavell has produced a "deconstructive reading of an American classic."[1] Howarth may have in mind those passages in which Cavell emphasizes Thoreau's commitment to writing rather than to speech. Like Derrida, Cavell's Thoreau not only opts for writing; he also apparently aligns it with distance, absence, and difference, even reading these qualities into speech acts that would seem to make us present to one another. "Speaking together face to face," Cavell notes (commenting on Thoreau), "can seem to deny that distance, to deny that facing one another requires acknowledging the presence of the other, revealing our positions, betraying them if need be. But to deny such things is to deny our separateness. And that makes us fictions of one another" (SW, 65). Writing presumably brings to light the "separateness" that conversation masks.

These resemblances to Derrida, however, occur in a context that deflects them. In *The Senses of Walden* each Derridean point begets its contrary, usually in a single sentence. Cavell writes, for example, that "the occurrence of a word is the occurrence of an object whose placement always has a point, and whose point always lies before and beyond it" (SW, 27). Here Cavell seems to affirm the deconstructive assumption that because no terms are intrinsically meaningful, meaning arises from their differences. But instead of endlessly deferring meaning, as Derrida's *différance* ends up doing, Cavell's statement relocates meaning. The point of a word neither resides in the word itself nor drifts in the spaces of the text. Rather, the point of the word "lies before and beyond it," in, among other things, the context that surrounds it and the language that makes it available. Cavell can accordingly go on to suggest that "writing, at its best, will come to a finish," to an end and a point of clarity, "in each mark of meaning, in each portion and sentence and word" (SW, 27). Instead of denying or embracing the meaning-as-difference dictum, Cavell thus completes it.

Far from offering a deconstructive reading of *Walden*, Cavell here adumbrates a powerful reading of deconstruction. I say adumbrates because in the preface to *The Senses of Walden* he disavows any intent of responding to deconstruction. As mentioned earlier, noting that he has been asked to relate Thoreau on writing to Derrida and Lévi-Strauss, Cavell replies, "I do not yet know or understand the pertinent views of these authors well enough to dispute or agree with them" (SW, xiv). Nevertheless, as the above example indicates, Cavell suggests a sympathetic, yet critical, response to Derrida, which I want to extend here.

SPEECH AND WRITING IN DERRIDA

Derrida's by now familiar ideas about writing and speech, already alluded to in chapter 3, do not need to be reviewed in detail here. His basic move—or at least the move that best

explains much of the criticism his work has thus far generated—involves finding in speech the qualities that Plato,
Rousseau, and other "logocentric" thinkers wish to place
outside it: absence, mediation, and spacing, to name only a
few. At stake in this move is not simply the purity of speech
but its philosophical function as an apparently indispensable guarantor of presence. In Rousseau and Lévi-Strauss,
for instance, speech preserves what Derrida calls a "pleni-
tude of meaning," a norm of direct, clear, authentic communication between neighbors present to themselves and
to each other "without difference, [in] a community of
speech where all the members are within earshot."[2] One
result of Derrida's deconstruction is not that neighbors turn
into strangers but that "strangers" loses its force in the
absence of any sure way of measuring or securing neigh-
borliness. For "neighbors" we can substitute clarity, truth,
presence, or any other positive term that speech presumably
safeguards. Derrida's writings, then, issue not in a direct
statement—such as, "We are all strangers to one another"—
but in a skeptical question: On what grounds can we claim
to know what something (or someone) says?

Numerous critics have tried to patch the distinction between speech and writing that Derrida deconstructs. These
critics, after defending the efficacy of speech, proceed to
find the qualities of speech in writing. Whereas Derrida
argues that difference, mediation, and signification make
speech as equivocal as writing, these critics maintain that
context, intent, and other controls make writing as determinate as speech.

The recent work of M. H. Abrams exemplifies this response to Derrida. In "How to Do Things with Texts,"
Abrams calls Derrida an "absolutist without absolutes."
Derrida, in this view, shares the assumption of the writers
he criticizes that "to be determinately understandable, language requires an absolute foundation," some rigorous, in-
disputable "transcendental signified," to put an end to the
otherwise infinite play of signification. But every allegedly
absolute foundation only extends the free play it would control. It follows that "since there is no such ground, there is
no stop to the play of undecidable meanings."[3]

Against this view, Abrams, citing the *Philosophical Investigations*, objects that "in practice language often works, that it gets its job done"[4] without the unimpeachable guarantees that Derrida thinks necessary to its success. By "practice" Abrams means everyday speech: "If one cannot share the joy, one can at least acknowledge the vertigo effected by Derrida's vision, yet take some reassurance in the thought that, even in a sign-world of absolute indeterminacy, it will presumably still be possible to achieve the 'effect' of telling a hawk from a handsaw, or the 'effect,' should the need arise, of identifying and warning a companion against an onrushing autobus."[5] Even without an invulnerable foundation, language works: alert to a very real onrushing bus, speakers warn their companions, who get out of the way.

For Abrams, writing can conserve and in some cases even reinforce the achievements of speech. In "The Deconstructive Angel," originally presented as a talk at an MLA symposium, Abrams again opposes to deconstruction his own "functional and pragmatic" linguistic theory based on the "ordinary use and experience of language."[6] By "ordinary use and experience" Abrams again means such speech acts as Lear's request "Pray you undo this button," one of many such examples noted in Abrams's paper. According to Abrams, even J. Hillis Miller, the deconstructionist whom he is debating, demonstrates in practice his lack of seriousness about deconstruction: "One of the games he [Miller] plays is that of a deconstructive critic of literary texts. The other is the game he will play in a minute or two when he steps out of his graphocentric premises onto this platform and begins to talk to us."[7] When Miller's talk is published, Abrams continues, the

> substitution of *écriture* for *parole* will certainly make a difference, but not an absolute difference; what Miller says here, that is, will not jump an ontological gap to the printed page, shedding on the way all the features that made it intelligible as discourse. For each of his readers will be able to reconvert the black-on-blanks back into speech, which he will hear in his mind's ear; he will perceive the words not simply as marks or sounds, but as already invested with meaning; also, by

immediate inference, he will be aware in his reading of an intelligent subject, very similar to the one we will infer while listening to him here, who organizes the well-formed and significant sentences and marshals the argument conveyed by the text.[8]

In fact, Abrams concludes, by employing "our ordinary skill and tact at language" as we read the essay, "we will understand it better than while hearing it in the mode of oral discourse, for the institution of print will render the fleeting words of his speech by a durable graphic correlate which will enable us to take our own and not the speaker's time in attending to it, as well as to re-read it, to collocate and to ponder until we are satisfied that we have approximated the author's meaning."[9] Writing, in short, works as well as speech, possibly even better, again without the sanctions that Derrida thinks necessary.

Abrams's comments illustrate one kind of response that skepticism usually excites—and always survives. I say this not to dismiss Abrams's critique but to indicate its limits. One problem is that Derrida concedes what Abrams alleges against him, namely, that in practice language achieves certain familiar effects. Derrida admits that if I shout, "Here comes a bus!" he will probably get out of the way. He agrees that in everyday life skeptical doubts seem "idle," to use Wittgenstein's phrase, or "cold, and strained, and ridiculous," to use Hume's.[10] Derrida is not maintaining that language fails or even that language only seems to work.[11] Instead, he is asking, how do we know when language works? Again to use Abrams's example, how do we know that we are to get out of the way? How can we be sure, or even sure enough, that this is the speaker's intent? What philosophical consequences follow from the fact that I usually get out of the way?

Meeting these questions head-on only leaves them in place. Affirming "I know what he means" (when he tells me to get out of the way) does not answer the question, *how* do you know? As Wittgenstein notes in *On Certainty,* "What is the proof that I *know* something? Most certainly not my saying I know it." "The queer thing," he continues, "is that even though I find it quite correct for someone to say 'Rub-

bish!' and so brush aside the attempt to confuse him with
doubts at bedrock,—nevertheless, I hold it to be incorrect
if he seeks to defend himself (using, e.g., the words 'I
know')."[12] From this vantage point, there is again something forced or unnatural about the skeptic's questions:
hence the legitimacy of replying "rubbish" and thus brush-
ing them aside; hence, I would add, the value of a response
like Abrams's. Nevertheless, one cannot bring out the limits
of skepticism by appealing to reactions that the skeptic
expects.

Writing and Presence in *The Senses of Walden*

Following an interpretation of Wittgenstein that finds significant parallels between ordinary-language philosophy
and Thoreau's Romanticism, Cavell spends much of *The
Senses of Walden* sympathetically developing Thoreau's reasons for writing. By writing (instead of speaking), Thoreau,
in this view, hopes to "make himself present to each circum-
stance, at every eventuality; since he is writing, in each significant mark" (SW, 61): "The written word, on a page, will
have to show that a particular man set it there, inscribed it,
chose and made the mark" (SW, 34). Similarly, "[Thoreau]
undertakes to make the word good. A true mathematical
reckoning of the sort he shows requires that every line be a
mark of honesty, that the lines be complete, omitting no expense or income, and that there be no mistake in the com-
putation" (SW, 30). As if that were not enough, Thoreau also
aims at a "wording of the world" that "will feel like a discovery of the *a priori*, a necessity of language, and of the world,
coming to light" (SW, 44). Finally, having established "his
mode of presence to the word," Thoreau wants to admit or
create "the reader's mode of presence to it. It [the written
word] is the ground upon which they will meet" (SW, 62).
Thoreau, in short, apparently entrusts to writing everything
Abrams entrusts to speech. Although both men use much
the same economic metaphor when they invest words with
meaning, Thoreau not only insists on writing his words,
he also drops Abrams's cautious talk of "approximating" a

speaker's meaning and "inferring" "an intelligent subject" from a text. (Abrams's comments here are vulnerable to the kinds of objections brought against the argument by analogy in chapter 3.) According to Cavell's reading, Thoreau will not countenance any mistake in computing meaning.

After Derrida, it is difficult to listen patiently to Thoreau's hopes, much less to endorse them. From this point of view, writing, Thoreau's means, seems painfully at odds with his ends. What Derrida calls "the spatial exteriority of the signifier," for example, or writing as a distant, material medium (like the type on this page), would seem to cripple Thoreau's desire to make himself present in any mark, let alone in every one. "The harsh law of spacing," again to quote Derrida, similarly fissures the words that Thoreau wants to complete or bring to a finish. In much the same way, the "iterability" or "citationality" of writing, its capacity to function in alien contexts, orphans it, undermining it as a ground upon which reader and writer may meet. Finally, the arbitrary link between signifier and signified makes writing a merely conventional code, not a means of uncovering the way the world must be. For all these reasons—and others I do not need to list here—writing seems to sabotage the aspirations that Thoreau entrusts to it.

If Cavell is right about *Walden,* none of these objections would come as any news to Thoreau. In Cavell's reading, Thoreau realizes that his words will reach us from a distance, if they even touch us:

> It is an accident, utterly contingent, that we should be present at these words [of *Walden*] at all. We feel this as the writer's withdrawal from the words on which he had staked his presence; and we feel this as the words' indifference to us, their disinterest in whether we choose to stay with them or not. (SW, 49)

"The succession of words is itself a rebuke" (SW, 61) to Thoreau's wish to make himself present in them, the chain of signifiers forever outracing his desire to contain it. Arriving at a "final reading" consequently seems "far off," maybe even impossible, because "once in [*Walden*], there seems no end; as soon as you have one word to cling to, it fractions or expands into others" (SW, 12–13), interminably dispersing the meaning that Thoreau wants to keep intact. Just as "the word's literality, its being just these letters, just here, rather than any others" (SW, 63) seems as contingent as Thoreau's retiring to Walden on the Fourth of July, there is only a chance that his writing will "have its effect; there is a good chance that it will not" (SW, 23).

Aware of these apparent obstacles in his way, Thoreau nevertheless chooses to write. He does not experiment with the appearance of words in order better to register his presence in them, as Blake sometimes is thought to have done in his illuminated printing.[13] He does not supplement his written words with gestures, say, or diagrams, but writes "absolutely," demonstrating "his faith [in writing] in the very act of marking the word" (SW, 29). Above all, he does not speak but criticizes "the fearful esotericism of his culture's parlance" (SW, xv), denigrates "language heard" as "transitory, a sound, a tongue, a dialect merely, almost brutish" (quoted in SW, 15), and notes that "speech is for the convenience of those who are hard of hearing" (quoted in SW, 64). Thoreau even models his own writing after mathematical notation in part because mathematics "exists *primarily* as notation; its point is not the fixing of a spoken language, which had preceded it, but the fixing of steps, which can thereby be remarked [i.e., marked again as well as noticed]" (SW, 31).

I emphasize Thoreau's commitment to writing not only because it seems to align him with Derrida—and thus create problems for Thoreau's strong commitment to presence—but also because it clashes with other tendencies in Romanticism as well as in Cavell's own work. At least in Wordsworth, the Romantic poet is a man speaking—not writing—to other people, typically comparing books to "barren leaves" at odds with "natural lore."[14] Cavell extends this emphasis of Romanticism in an essay significantly entitled "Must We Mean What We Say?" (say, not write). Answering some criticisms of ordinary-language philosophy, Cavell objects that "the philosopher, understandably, often takes the isolated man bent silently over a book as his model for what using language is. But the primary fact of natural language is that it is something spoken, spoken

together" (MWM, 33). Wittgenstein's well-known formulation—"To imagine a language is to imagine a form of
life"—accordingly implies that "philosophy needs to take
instruction here, that it tends to imagine language dead, no
longer spoken" (WPT, 9). Along similar lines in *The Claim of
Reason*, Cavell speaks sympathetically of Freud's insight that
"the human individual, to win freedom, must be something
that can fight for recognition, which now means, vie with
its incorporated interpretations of itself for a voice, for the
leading voice, in its history" (CR, 474). Thoreau's affirmation of writing thus needs to be squared not only with his
own interest in making himself and the world present but
also with Cavell's apparently Wordsworthian emphasis on
speech.

According to Cavell, Thoreau opts for writing not despite
its remoteness but because of it. Everything that I have cited
against writing as a means of ensuring presence—its reaching us from a distance, for example, and its "literality"—
ends up in its favor. Explaining how Thoreau turns the
apparent disadvantages of writing into strengths—in effect,
how he converts "outwardness" into an "opportunity"
(SW, 55)—involves Cavell in several overlapping paradoxes:
to meet his readers, Thoreau has to withdraw from them; to
establish himself as a neighbor, he must become a stranger;
to get his readers to open their mouths, he must refuse to
speak; to return a word to his readers, he must withhold it
from them; to orient his countrymen, he must get them lost;
to enforce their presence to his words, he must secure their
distance from them; to affirm his inhabiting or settling down
at Walden, he must leave it; to overcome words, he must
use them; to earn his life, he must spend it—"only so does
one save it" (SW, 45).

As a first step toward unraveling these riddles, I want to
point out some similarities between Thoreau's actions and
the Ancient Mariner's, as analyzed by Cavell in his reading
of Coleridge's poem. Disputing Robert Penn Warren's suggestion that "the Mariner is received back into the world of
men," Cavell notes that

> he is not enabled to participate in that world on equal
> terms with others. To the extent that the Mariner is
> not recovered to the world of men, the country to

which he returns (our world) *remains* dramatized, dia-
grammed, by the cold country he has survived. Otherwise, why should his penance be to proclaim to its
inhabitants, ever and anon and from land to land,
the identical moral he had to learn in order to survive
his life-in-death? The difference in the countries is
that above the line [crossed by the Mariner on his voy-
age] the inhabitants are able to conceal their rejection
of the world, and for the most part or, say, for practical purposes, to adjust to their condition as if it were
the ordinary condition of the world. To bring them
back from their concealed life-in-death, accordingly,
the Mariner has to break into their adjustments, to become a disturber of their peace, which is no peace.
(IQO, 199–200)

The Mariner disturbs his contemporaries' peace—in this
case the Wedding Guest's participation in a wedding festi-
val—not simply by breaking into the Wedding Guest's life
but by getting the Wedding Guest to speak first, much as
Thoreau, in order to get his readers to open their mouths,
must initially refuse to speak. The tale that the Mariner goes
on to tell, moreover, depicts his isolation and wandering. To
meet his readers, Thoreau, too, has had to separate from
them: he sees himself as traveler or stranger writing to his
"kindred from a distant land" (SW, 54). In competing with
the marriage feast that the Wedding Guest wants to attend,
the Mariner's tale suggests that the intimacy supposedly secured by marriage or by participating in a wedding feast is
no intimacy precisely because it has bypassed the Mariner's
experience—the experience of drifting "alone on a wide
wide sea" that he relates to the Wedding Guest. According
to Thoreau, too, intimacy depends in part on sincerity, defined by Cavell (paraphrasing Thoreau) as "the capacity to
live one's own separateness, to sail the Atlantic and Pacific
Ocean of one's being alone" (SW, 54). (In Emerson's "Fate,"
as Cavell interprets it in "The Melodrama of the Unknown
Woman: A Reading of *Gaslight*,"[15] Emerson takes a similarly
bleak view of public intimacy, aligning marriage as it now
stands with adultery.) Finally, having told his tale, the Mariner leaves the Wedding Guest "stunned," much as Thoreau
will leave a reader like Emerson wretched and nervous, feel-

ing deprived of something (and thus "sadder" [l. 623]) but in search of something else (and thus "wiser" [l. 624])—genuine intimacy and peace, say, and not the superficial togetherness tolerated by society in its present form.

There are, of course, some obvious differences between the Ancient Mariner and Thoreau: for one thing, the Wedding Guest "cannot choose but hear" (l. 18), whereas Cavell emphasizes that Thoreau's readers are apparently freer to leave. But the similarities between the two figures should also be kept in mind, lest Thoreau seem exempt from the desperation and confusion he sees in his readers. At one point Cavell describes the Ancient Mariner as "more a patient than a doctor, more a symptom than a cure" (IQO, 201) in part because he leaves the Wedding Guest "awaiting redemption" and not yet achieving it. I would say that Cavell's Thoreau is a patient as well as a doctor whose cure is similarly open-ended. Everything he diagnoses in his readers he must constantly heal in himself.

According to Thoreau, again as Cavell portrays him, we —the readers he wants to help—think we know where (and who) we are, but we are lost. We think we are being practical but we are wasting our lives. We think we are awake but we are dreaming. In Cavell's words:

> We take one thing for another in every field of thought and in every mode of action. . . . We do not see our hand in what happens, so we call certain events melancholy accidents when they are the inevitabilities of our projects, and we call other events necessities because we will not change our minds. (SW, 81–82)

More specifically, we put slavery at a distance, not realizing that we are slaves; or we are interested only in the far-off and the exotic, not realizing that "*next* to us the grandest laws are continually being executed" (quoted in SW, 77).

It follows that the "first step in attending to our education is to observe the strangeness of our lives, our estrangement from ourselves, the lack of necessity in what we profess to be necessary" (SW, 55). Before we can choose a saner way of life, we have to see that we have chosen the desperate one we accept as inevitable. The paradoxes mentioned earlier all result from Thoreau's prodding us into taking this first step and thus making us see "our hand in what we choose to say"—and do (SW, 67). To confront his readers, for example, he moves away from them, not to distance himself from them but to bring out the distance already there. By turning to the woods, where he is "better known," he is challenging his readers' everyday, unearned assumption that they know him, that his place is with them. As Cavell puts it, "The writer has secrets to tell which can only be told to strangers. Only those who recognize themselves as strangers can be told them, because those who think themselves familiars will think they have already heard what the writer is saying" (SW, 92–93). By removing himself from his readers, Thoreau is not exchanging intimacy for loneliness but exposing the separateness that their so-called life together veils.[16]

Cavell suggests that several stylistic devices in *Walden*—in particular, its "puns and paradoxes, its fracturing of idiom and twisting of quotation, its drones of fact and flights of impersonation" (SW, 16)—accordingly aim not at confusing us but at uncovering our confusion. Instead of inventing new words, Thoreau plays with the words we use every day: "interest," "practical," "rich," "own," and "profit," among many others.[17] By playing with these words, he tries to pry them loose from the impoverished meanings we have assigned them. As Cavell explains,

> Our words have for us the meaning we give to them. As our lives stand, the meaning we give them is rebuked by the meaning they have in our language—the meaning, say, that writers live on, the meaning we also, in moments, know they have but which mostly remains a mystery to us. Thoreau is doing with our ordinary assertions what Wittgenstein does with our more patently philosophical assertions—bringing them back to a context in which they are alive. It is the appeal from ordinary language to itself; a rebuke of our lives by what we may know of them, if we will. (SW, 92)

By emphasizing will here, Thoreau is assuming that "our mind is chanced, but not forced, by language" (SW, 67); we therefore can—and should—"assess our orientation or position to what we say" (SW, 67).[18] And orientation, Cavell continues, is a matter of

> bearings, of the ability to keep a course and to move in natural paths from any point to any other. The depths of the book are nothing apart from its surfaces. Figurations of language can be thought of as ways of reflecting the surfaces and depths of a word onto one another. (SW, 65)

By construing "practicality," for example, in exclusively financial terms, we think we have hit the bottom of the word when in fact we have only skimmed its surface. Thoreau's "figurations of language" are not meant to adorn the literal meaning of a word but to unsettle it by plumbing its unacknowledged depths, in this case exposing "the mysticism of what society thinks practical" (SW, 90).[19]

Cavell links Thoreau's wordplay to Wittgenstein's but I want to make an even more unlikely comparison between Thoreau's punning and Groucho Marx's.[20] As Cavell puts it: "Groucho's commitment to the pun is a profound trait of his character not because his puns are always funny (often they are not), but because it is a commitment, a pure commitment to *his* response, refusing the coin of what the world has given him to mean. Thus is humor a moral equivalent of heroism" (TS, 134). In Thoreau's case, refusing the coin of the world—say, by withholding a word like "practical" from circulation and playing with it, turning it over or inside out—is a means toward returning to the word meanings we currently neglect. Turning words from their everyday usage in order to return them correlates with Thoreau's wanting to "[turn] us around, and so [lose] us" (SW, 50) and thus shake our sense that we know where we are. Reading *Walden* accordingly recalls Thoreau's own claim that "'you only need sit still long enough in some attractive spot in the wood that all its inhabitants may exhibit themselves to you by turns'— i.e., in succession, and by turning" (SW, 48), much like Thoreau's own tropes, or turns of phrase. Along surprisingly similar lines, contemporary literary theorists speak of tropes turning words from their literal or referential use. But for a critic like de Man "the turning motion of tropes" endlessly spins words out of control, ensuring our disorientation and consequent inability to stop the dizzying dissemination of meaning.[21] For Thoreau, by contrast, such turning, or troping, is not an end in itself but a means of returning to words the meanings we refuse to let them have.

Thoreau's playing with words thus breaks the circuit of communication only to strengthen it. More generally, Cavell has written that "what makes metaphor unnatural is its occasion to transcend our criteria; not as if to repudiate them, as if they are arbitrary; but to expand them [as Thoreau does with 'practical'], as though they are contracted. . . . In the realm of the figurative, our words are not felt as confining but as releasing, or not as binding but as bonding" (BOGE, 94)—bonding those who feel released, who get the joke or the pun. Although one "*can* get along in the everyday world without exercising the capacity for the figurative," doing so "will debar you from certain other intimacies," maybe, if we go by a text like *Walden,* from intimacy per se (BOGE, 95–96).

Thoreau's commitment to writing, like his penchant for wordplay, thus follows from his desire to plunge his readers into what they usually avoid. The "spatial exteriority" of print, far from compromising Thoreau's purposes, accordingly furthers them:

> The reader's position has been specified as that of the stranger. To write to him is to acknowledge that he is outside the words, at a bent arm's length, and alone with the book; that his presence to these words is perfectly contingent, and the choice to stay with them continuously his own; that they are his points of departure and origin. (SW, 63)

By writing, Thoreau has put his readers exactly where he wants them: outside the writer that they think they know; alone with the words that social pressures distort or constrict; "at a bent arm's length" from the book they are studying, with the hand they have in reading *Walden*—in holding it and turning its pages—dramatizing the hand they have in upholding the "perfectly contingent" historical arrangements they deem necessary.[22] Speech, by contrast, reinforces the illusion of familiarity that Thoreau wants to puncture. As Cavell observes in the passage cited earlier, "speaking together face to face" can seem to annul the distance Thoreau wants to preserve.

In labeling the words of *Walden* our "points of departure and origin," Cavell is recalling that Thoreau leaves us, just as he leaves Walden and just as we leave him.[23] Thoreau spends much of *Walden* championing leave-taking, withdrawal, abandonment, going on, exploring, traveling, experimenting, progressing, and the consequent impossibility of arresting the "successiveness of words" or ending one's work, whether writing, building, or hoeing. Yet he also values integrity, constancy, hardness, meeting, finding one's footing, settling down, reaching bottom, inhabiting, stillness, sitting, writing that comes "to a finish," lines that are "complete," marks that honestly register a writer's continuous presence, and reading that comes to an end. Perhaps the deepest paradox that Cavell unearths in *Walden* is that leaving is not simply compatible with meeting and settling down but necessary to them.

Forbidding someone else's departure, in other words, precludes our meeting him by negating his autonomy, his separateness, thus making him a fiction.[24] For Thoreau, this scenario is not just a hypothetical possibility but characterizes the stunted everyday affairs of his countrymen. Again, "we think that our current necessities are our final ones. We have defined our lives in front" (SW, 73). We consequently find ourselves frozen into habitual postures of specious intimacy, like mannequins who lock arms but never embrace. That is our tragedy, one cause of tragedy being that "we would rather murder the world than permit it to expose us to change" (MWM, 351). "Murder" here does not describe something exotic but something we do to ourselves and to each other every day. Our desperation is quiet but still suicidal as well as homicidal (again illustrating the necessary reflexiveness of spiritual torture): hence the various "postures of perpetual penance, or self-mortification" described by Thoreau in his opening pages (BOGE, 106). Quiet desperation in Thoreau resembles "silent melancholy" in Emerson, "savage torpor" in Wordsworth, and "dejection" in

Coleridge. All of these states result in part from our refusal
to take an interest in our experience; all are fatal to the
thinker as well as to the objects of thought (Emerson even
goes so far as to conclude that "we mostly do not exist,
but haunt the world, ghosts of ourselves" [MUW, 39]), like
the ghastly crew that includes the Ancient Mariner).[25] For
Cavell, Thoreau, like these other Romantics, is brave not
only in noting the everyday reality of death-in-life but in
affirming the possibility of life-in-death, a possibility that
depends on the willingness to change, "to continue to be
born, to be natal, hence mortal" (IQO, 224).

Thoreau accordingly leaves Walden ready to improvise
because he is "undefined in front," with "several more lives
to live," his plans indefinite (SW, 45). (I say "improvise" to
tie the conclusion of *Walden* to the comedies of remarriage,
as discussed in chapter 4.) His dwelling is not a fort where
he will be forever secure or always exempt from the kind of
crisis that brought him to Walden (this is another sign of his
bravery). Instead of learning to prevent risk, he has learned
to welcome it, "to allow the world to change, and to learn
change from it, to permit it strangers, accepting its own
strangeness" (SW, 119). Leaving Walden does not negate the
value of his having stayed there. We admittedly cannot see
an end to our labors, whether we are building, writing, or
reading. Yet they are not for that reason pointless. Similarly,
we cannot know in advance when a reading will feel complete, when a line of writing will come to a finish, when a
turn of phrase returns a word to us, or when a dwelling will
work. But such uncertainty, instead of undermining our
tasks, humanizes them. By thus spending our lives, we save
them—from the stultifying security (the quiet desperation
or savage torpor) that shuns risks as well as from the paralyzing despair that lets the endlessness of our pursuits nullify them.

> Our first resolve should be toward the nextness of the
> self to the self; it is that capacity not to deny either of
> its positions or attitudes—that it is the watchman or
> guardian of itself, and hence demands of itself trans-
> parence, settling, clearing, constancy; and that it is the
> workman whose eye cannot see to the end of its labors,

but whose answerability is endless for the construc-
tions in which it houses itself. (SW, 109)[26]

Neither a fixed possession nor an airy nothing, "having a
self" is thus a "continuous *activity*"—like reaching bottom,
settling down, accepting the world, or reading *Walden*.

Or speaking. Instead of giving up on speech, Thoreau is
trying to show that serious speech demands the continuous
interpretive efforts required by his prose. He is suggesting
that if writing seems to be peculiarly problematic—because
less immediate or direct than speech—that may be because
speaking does not seem problematic enough.[27] He holds out
the hope that we may be "capable of serious speech again,"
which means capable of allowing "our lives and our language . . . their full range and autonomy" (SW, 34). Instead
of contradicting Cavell's commitment to speech, Thoreau's
choice of writing thus interprets it: Cavell affirms not simply
speech but the recovery of speech from our everyday "voice-
lessness," from the muting of our voices by what Emerson
calls conformity.[28]

THE SENSES OF WALDEN AND DECONSTRUCTION

In the hope of clarifying a subtle text, I have obviously de-
ferred highlighting the relevance of *The Senses of Walden* to
the debate on deconstruction with which I began. Readers
who expect the preceding account to pay off in a final solution to skepticism will be disappointed. One moral of *The
Senses of Walden*, in fact, is that skepticism outlasts, even
feeds off, the attempt to end it. In any seemingly airtight
attack on skepticism, the skeptic can find holes.

I do not mean to hint that Abrams, in the essays mentioned earlier, wishes to refute skepticism once and for all.
But the examples he cites against Derrida and Miller presup-
pose what they wish to question. It is difficult not to construe Abrams's anecdote in the following optimistic way: a
speaker—already safely identified as a companion—clearly
warns that a bus is coming. I, of course, know that I must
get out of the way.

Following Cavell's treatment of Thoreau, we can say that Derrida is right to question whether we know, or must do, any such thing. There is a film of necessity, familiarity, and assurance about Abrams's story that needs to be brushed away. From the point of view developed in *The Senses of Walden*, Derrida, then, does not go too far, as his critics often suppose; he does, however, stop too soon. The fact that intimacy (or communication) does not depend on knowledge admittedly leaves it in doubt. But the problematic status of intimacy defines it as human, or points to what human intimacy entails: trust, choice, risk, and continuous effort, among other things. Instead of subverting or vitiating human relationships, open-endedness thus characterizes them. In having uncertainty constitute rather than undermine our relationships, Cavell is characteristically working toward "an acknowledgment of human limitation which does not leave us chafed by our own skin" (MWM, 61). The Romantics' "acceptance of the sufficiency of human finitude" again indicates what Cavell sees as their bravery.

Facing up to our limitations sounds like common sense, but Cavell, or for that matter Thoreau, is not replacing skepticism with our everyday beliefs about human nature and the world. As he explains in an essay on Emerson:

> It is not quite right to say that we *believe* the world exists (though certainly we should not conclude that we do *not* believe this, that we *fail* to believe its existence), and wrong even to say we *know* it exists (while of course it is equally wrong to say we fail to know this). . . . [O]ur relation to the world's existence is somehow *closer* than the ideas of believing and knowing are made to convey. (SW, 145)

In case this seems like a trivial or merely semantic point, I want to cite a recent essay by Stanley Fish, who argues that

> in order to make even the simplest of assertions or perform the most elementary action, I must already be proceeding in the context of innumerable beliefs which cannot be the object of my attention, because they are the content of my attention: beliefs on the order of the identity of persons, the existence of animate and inani-

mate entities, the stability of objects, in addition to the countless beliefs that underwrite the possibility and intelligibility of events in my local culture—beliefs that give me, without reflection, a world populated by streets, sidewalks, telephone poles, restaurants, figures of authority and figures of fun, worthy and unworthy tasks, achievable and unachievable goals, and so on.[29]

According to Cavell, "believing in" the existence of animate and inanimate entities smacks of "believing in" a story about which there may be some doubt. "Believing in" the existence of things and people—like Abrams's talk of inferring or approximating a speaker's intent—thus removes us from the intimacy with the world suggested by Thoreau's metaphor of our neighboring the world or Cavell's claim that we acknowledge it. "Neighboring the world," "acknowledging it," and being "next" to it (in Emerson) try to capture the feeling "that my relation to the existence of the world, or to my existence in the world, is not given in words but in silence" (SW, 145)—in what I do and not simply in what I know or believe. As Cavell goes on to explain, silence here is not "a matter of keeping your mouth shut but of understanding when, and how, not to yield to the temptation to say what you do not or cannot exactly mean" (SW, 145)—the temptation to say, for example, that "I believe in the solidity of matter and therefore I will open the door rather than attempt to walk through the walls," to cite another example from Fish's essay.

Cavell, then, is not denying skepticism but reconceiving it, or shifting its weight, to borrow a phrase from *The Claim of Reason* (CR, 45). The temptation to refute skepticism—by asserting, for example, "I know X exists"—accedes to the skeptic's obsession with knowledge, an obsession that Cavell wants to interpret, or derive, not satisfy. Cavell thus agrees with the skeptic that "we cannot know the world exists." But for Cavell this means "its presentness to us cannot be a function of knowing. The world is to be *accepted*; as the presentness of other minds is not to be known, but acknowledged" (MWM, 324), another insight he takes from Thoreau's Romanticism as well as from Wittgenstein.[30] Shifting the weight of the skeptic's argument involves reconceiving its threat. Our problem again becomes accepting the world, not (simply) knowing it.

I can more specifically show how Cavell's reading of *The Senses of Walden* bears on deconstruction by contrasting Cavell's book to Walter Benn Michaels's "*Walden*'s False Bottoms," a powerful deconstructive reading of *Walden* that deserves the praise Jonathan Culler and other critics have given it. I use "deconstructive" rather loosely here. Michaels nowhere mentions Derrida but his reading nonetheless extends Derrida's uneasiness with hierarchical oppositions, one reason for Culler's citing Michaels as an instance of deconstructive criticism.[31] Michaels aims at recuperating the "wretchedness" and "nervousness" many readers—Emerson among them—have felt in reading *Walden*. In his view, the discomfort excited by *Walden* results from Thoreau's subverting the ground on which he asks the reader to stand. Even as Thoreau urges us to touch bottom, he unsettles each seemingly solid ground we touch, be it nature, writing, or figurative language. Little wonder, Michaels concludes, we feel wretched and nervous: "*Walden* insists upon the necessity for such a search [for a sure foundation] at the same time that it dramatizes the theoretical impossibility of succeeding in it."[32]

According to Michaels, modern critics have tried to defuse the anxiety that *Walden* excites. Assuming the organic unity of literary works, the New Critics, for example, acknowledged Thoreau's paradoxes, ambiguities, and contradictions only to resolve them. What an earlier generation of critics called Thoreau's personal faults—his lapses in judgment, say, or forgetfulness—the New Critics redeemed as his text's virtues, its "apparent inconsistencies pointing toward final literary (i.e., not necessarily logical) truths."[33] Although Cavell grants the text its loose ends, in Michaels's view he nevertheless gives the reader the power to tie them in a "visionary union" that Michaels wants to unravel. Instead of questioning the resolution of Thoreau's antinomies, Cavell relocates it, claiming for the reader's experience of *Walden* what the New Critics claimed for *Walden* itself.

It seems to me that Michaels exaggerates the serenity of Cavell's reader. Following Thoreau, Cavell's reader does not conclusively resolve crises but spends a lifetime (daily) resolving them. For Michaels, the fact that each resolution comes undone ironically cancels its value, leaving the reader "to participate always in an act of foundation or interpretation which is inevitably arbitrary—there is as much to be said against it as there is for it."[34] But for Cavell the provisional character of our resolutions marks them as human; they are not everything we might wish but something nevertheless. Instead of plunging us into a quandary, Cavell's Thoreau involves us in never-ending, but purposeful, activity that makes Michaels's conclusion seem as static as the neatly tied New Critical resolution that he rightly dislikes.[35] Because we never really settle down, Michaels seems to argue, we get nowhere. He accordingly leaves us stuck, spinning our wheels, never gripping anything solid, much like the external-world skeptic staring hard, but ineffectually, at the generic object. Because we never really settle down, Cavell suggests, we are always settling down. He leaves us in motion—or in history—always needing to make, and often making, something solid enough to use. Although our labors can never be finished, we are nevertheless responsible for finishing them as best as we can. "As best as we can" is neither a fixed norm we can know in advance nor an empty category but a guideline we are forever (re)constructing.

I return one last time to Thoreau's bravery, further described by Cavell as Thoreau's willingness not to let his leaving undermine "his responsibility in living as he has, staying where he has stayed, saying what he has (so far) said." Thoreau, he continues, knows all about "the mutual interference or dependence of words, their reaches out of our control, and yet [knows] that there is something to say *now*, something there is no time in which to hedge or amplify in all the ways it *could* be, might have to be, something therefore inherently *unguarded*, something whose guarding must come to an end (if you are to deliver yourself of an utterance, a sentence, a 'complete' thought). Not to let the necessities of dwelling (for a time) and of leaving (in time) deny another—that [is] the mark of honesty," and another sign of Thoreau's courage (letter, August 6, 1984).

In these first five chapters I have sketched the background against which I want to place Cavell's comments and essays on contemporary criticism. Romanticism does not so much complete the picture, like a missing puzzle piece, as inform all its details. In looking at Cavell's Romanticism, I have not brought up something new but brought out something that shapes his approach to skepticism from the beginning. Having described this approach, I turn now to the remarks on contemporary theory that grow out of it.

6

LITERARY THEORY AND THE FLIGHT FROM THE ORDINARY

CAVELL'S HESITATION in responding to Fish, de Man, and Derrida partly results from the difficulty he has experienced in reading their work. I think he finds their work difficult because it seems so like his own and yet so distant. Especially in Derrida, he can see some aspects of himself: a concern for the literary dimensions of philosophical writing, for example, and a willingness to quarrel with academic philosophy.[1] But each of these similarities, as well as others that I will be discussing, takes on a different cast in Derrida's thought, rendering his work alien as well as sympathetic. Cavell accordingly finds the gap separating him from Derrida—and American from French intellectual life—"maddeningly unscalable, too near to ignore, too far to go" (MUW, 32).

The scattered remarks that I am about to examine result from Cavell's ambivalence toward Derrida's work and much contemporary literary theory. I will focus here on a few of these comments, in particular Cavell's uneasiness with the portrait of Austin sketched by de Man and Fish; his refusal to call binary, hierarchical oppositions "undecidable"; and his conviction that traditional philosophy or "metaphysics" is best discussed in terms of emptiness rather than presence. These brushes with recent theory not only grow out of the response to skepticism that I have been discussing but clarify it.

AUSTIN AND ''UNDECIDABLE'' OPPOSITIONS

I start with Austin because Cavell so often does, not just in responding to recent criticism but in declaring the origins of his own work. (*The Claim of Reason,* for instance, is dedicated to Thompson Clarke and to the memory of J. L. Austin.) In "The Politics of Interpretation," Cavell's first published encounter with contemporary literary theory, he objects to Fish's claim that Austin distinguishes "ordinary" from literary language, a distinction that Fish goes on to dispute. For Cavell, ordinary language in Austin offsets philosophical, not literary, language: "the errors or discrepancies or follies his appeals to ordinary language immediately counter are ones that philosophizing is apt to produce" (TS, 37). Philosophizing produces these follies when it turns words like "part" and "all" from their ordinary usage, asking about an object fully in view "But do you see all of it? Isn't part of it hidden?" to use an example from my second chapter.

Austin's respect for how we ordinarily use words grows out of a vision of language that Cavell thinks Fish misconstrues. In *Is There a Text in This Class?*, Fish puts Austin's view this way: "When we communicate, it is because we are parties to a set of discourse agreements which are in effect decisions as to what can be stipulated as a fact" (quoted in TS, 40). Although Cavell shares a sense of agreement underlying communication, he objects that

> Fish's words here make this agreement seem much more, let me say, sheerly conventional than would seem plausible if one were considering other regions of Austin's work, for example, the region of excuses, where the differences, for one small instance, between doing something mistakenly, accidentally, heedlessly, carelessly, inadvertently, automatically, thoughtlessly, inconsiderately, and so on are worked out with unanticipated clarity and completeness but where the more convinced you are by the results, the less you will feel like attributing them to agreements that are expressible as decisions. How could we have agreed to consequences of our words that we are forever in the process of unearthing, consequences that with each turn seem further to unearth the world? (TS, 40)

Cavell once again wants to vindicate what he calls the naturalness of ordinary language while acknowledging its conventionality. As I put it in chapter 3, for him our mutual attunement is too intricate and deep to have resulted from some prior decision.

Although Fish's conventionalist account of language may not fit Austin, or may fit only one of Austin's emphases, it reappears in the work of de Man and other critics, encouraging their feeling that crucial distinctions are undecidable. "Undecidable" does not mean that in practice we lump together hawks and handsaws, or accidents and mistakes. It does mean that we determine such differences only according to merely local or conventional criteria. Although we may call our decisions objective, factual, rational, or natural, they are not. Each of these terms confers a spurious legitimacy and necessity on judgments that are at bottom arbitrary or, what becomes the same thing, founded on self-serving community agreements.

In commenting on de Man and Fish, Cavell brings up several such distinctions:

constative/performative
referential/nonreferential
natural/conventional
ordinary (or everyday)/queer (or strange)
serious/ridiculous
speech/writing
reality/dream
original/quoted
individuality/conformity
grammar/rhetoric
knives/forks

In de Man, undoing any one of these distinctions, even an apparently trivial or neutral one like knives/forks, points the way toward unraveling them all. In each case, the alleged secondariness or derivativeness of the term on the right ends up infecting the left one. Take original/quoted: because all words are learned and thus (re)cited, none can be stigmatized as quoted or privileged as original. Similarly, because you can do with a fork what you can do with a knife (cut food, for instance, or even spread butter), no stable distinction can be drawn between them. Finally, nothing in the grammar of a question or any other speech act (e.g., "Isn't this fun?") settles its rhetorical function or determines whether we should take it as a request or as a rhetorical question, to name two of many possibilities.

Cavell's approach to one of de Man's best known examples—Archie Bunker's replying "What's the difference?" when his wife Edith asks him whether he wants his bowling shoes laced over or under—shows why he bristles at calling binary oppositions undecidable. According to de Man, Archie's response looks like a request for information: his wife at least construes it that way when she replies to his (apparent) question by patiently explaining the difference between lacing over and under. But "What's the difference?" also can be taken as denying that there is any difference, or any difference that merits explaining: Archie's impatience with his wife's discussion of the difference shows that he means his question this way. The humor in the scene results from Archie and his wife being at cross-purposes with no obvious way of resolving their misunderstanding. Edith's patience provokes Archie's irritation, which in turn leads her to amplify the very explanation that he does not want. De Man concludes his analysis of the scene by observing that "the same grammatical pattern engenders two meanings that are mutually exclusive: the literal meaning asks for the concept (difference) whose existence is denied by the figurative meaning" (quoted in TS, 43). The tension between grammar and rhetoric here renders the meaning of Archie's question undecidable.

Language thus seems untamable to de Man, even perverse, in its ability to thwart a speaker's intentions. De Man echoes Derrida here, who similarly derives what he calls "the anguish of writing" from

> the necessarily restricted passageway of speech against which all possible meanings push each other, preventing each other's emergence. Preventing, but calling upon each other, provoking each other too, unforeseeably and as if despite oneself, in a kind of autonomous overassemblage of meanings, a power of pure equivocality that makes the creativity of the classical God appear all too poor. Speaking frightens me because, by never saying enough, I also say too much.[2]

The uncontrollable equivocality of speech renders our agreeing on the meaning of an expression either a fantastic accident or the result of coercion, of Archie, say, bullying Edith into admitting she was "wrong."

Cavell resists this pessimistic conclusion, arguing "you might as well say it is perverse or aberrant of the normally functioning human hand that it can grasp, and make a fist, play arpeggios, and shade the eyes, and be held up to bless or to swear" (TS, 43)—you might as well say this, in other words, as say that because one and the same grammatical pattern can serve different rhetorical functions, language is out of control and meaning undecidable. Or perhaps, Cavell continues, using a question for constative purposes is best compared to using a fist to play arpeggios. But "then it should be cause for amazement that so many people, and so young, with no special history of side-show virtuosity, can negotiate rhetorical questions so smoothly" (TS, 44), something they could not do if rhetorical questions were as forced, or unnatural, as fist-played arpeggios.

What de Man sees as the unruliness of language Cavell sees as its practical resourcefulness, its adaptability to the many demands we put on it. Because of the flexibility of language, speaking admittedly involves risks: we cannot know in advance whether a given grammatical pattern will achieve a desired rhetorical effect. We are always having to wonder whether we have said enough, too much, or the right thing, to name only a few possibilities. But speaking also involves decisions and responsibilities: we are always having to stand by what we say or take it back, again to mention only two of many choices. Cavell reads Archie's question ("What's the difference?") as "a hedge against assertion" (TS, 44). Like a rhetorical question ("Wasn't that a great film?"), it asks for a response but not necessarily for information. In this scene, it is not clear what Archie wants from his wife—not clear to her or to him. But this indeterminacy, in addition to being a source of humor, "is a fact about some Archie, not about the inevitable relation between grammar and rhetoric. The moral of the example [is] that there is no inevitable relation between them" (TS, 45). Grammar, Cavell concludes, "cannot, or ought not, of itself dictate what you mean, what it is up to you to say" (TS, 45).

The function of Archie's question thus is not so much undecidable as it is up to Archie and Edith to decide by talking, shouting, or doing whatever else their relationship permits.

The possibilities are limitless, or limited only by the give-and-take of their marriage. Cavell balks at de Man's use of "undecidable" partly because he wants to expand, or keep open, what we decide. Grammar will not take the interpretation of a statement out of our hands—and here Cavell agrees with de Man—but that does not mean the statement is unreadable. Instead, it means that we have to read it and take responsibility for how we construe it.

The example I have been discussing concerns a couple for whom reading one another is a repetitive, everyday task, as uneventful as getting ready to go bowling. The meaning of Archie's question is neither instantly, unequivocally clear nor determinable once and for all. It is subject to debate, denial, explanation, and whatever else he and his wife decide to engage in. Archie's explanations, or his evasions, may come to an end but only at a definite point and for specific reasons (his impatience, his friends' readiness to go, and so on). Breaking off an explanation has its consequences as does prolonging one or embarking on one at the right time or too soon. But what counts as breaking off or prolonging an explanation, as well as the consequences that these acts entail, is for Archie and his wife to decide.

I have been emphasizing what these two individuals (have to) determine not just once but every day. I have stayed with Cavell's reading of Archie and Edith Bunker because it involves marriage, or domestic life, repetition and the everyday, key terms in Cavell's response to skepticism. Cavell defines skepticism by its disappointment in daily life or its necessarily frustrated "drive to reach the unconditioned" (DK, 17), to arrive at some absolute foundation for our judgments, thereby stripping "ourselves of the responsibility we have in meaning [or in failing to mean] one thing, or one way, rather than another" (BOGE, 311). From the skeptic's point of view, repetition smacks of failure, or irony; it suggests our inability to get things right once and for all.

In response, Cavell, following Wittgenstein and Thoreau, urges us to "cleave to the everyday" (TS, 9), that is, to bring words back, or home, to the language games in which they are ordinarily used. Bringing words back to our everyday use of them in turn means letting words live, or reattaching their meaning to the flow of language.[3] The skeptic longs to fix words, to freeze their meaning, as Wittgenstein suggests when he remarks that the skeptic puts us "on to slippery ice where there is no friction and so in a certain sense the conditions are ideal" (*Philosophical Investigations*, no. 107).[4] But, Wittgenstein continues, "just because of that, we are unable to walk." The skeptic's necessarily unsatisfiable craving for clarity—here, for the absence of roughness and friction in communication—thus ends up paralyzing him. Against the skeptic's longing for some ironclad connection between words and meaning, say between grammar and rhetoric, Cavell opposes the admittedly uneven ground of our everyday life together. While forcing us occasionally to stumble (for example, in reading one another), this roughness nevertheless allows us to walk, walking (for Kierkegaard and Thoreau) being "the gait of finitude" (WPC, 22). Walking suggests Cavell's desire not only to put words in motion but to "de-sublimize" or "diurnalize" their meaning, to let interpretation be bound up with something as pedestrian as walking. For Cavell, interpretations of statements thus "come to an end, somewhere, each in its time and place, to be discovered philosophically, let us say, time after time, place by place" (DT, 531) and skepticism gives way "to the acceptance of a repetition that includes endless specific succumbings to the conditions of skepticism and endless specific recoveries from it" (DK, 30). Instead of answering skeptical doubts, we thus undo them, "repeatedly, unmelodramatically, uneventfully" (WPC, 40). We learn to "live with stumbling" (IQO, 184) as the condition for walking at all. Instead of scanning the heavens for answers, Cavell is typically advising us to look beneath our feet (WPC, 4), even as we walk or lace our shoes.

Metaphysics as Emptiness

I have been stressing how Cavell wants to let the meaning of words depend on the everyday decisions of the people using them. I seem to have forgotten his equally strong reluctance to ground our judgments in "agreements that are expressible as decisions," to return to the statement on

Austin already cited. Cavell's arguing for the necessity, even the naturalness, of our criteria leads me to another dimension of deconstructive theory that makes him uneasy.

Derrida, as Cavell reads him, aims at deconstructing "metaphysics," in particular its claim that universals or essences, for example, exist beyond language. From this point of view, metaphysics is tied to assertions of presence; it peoples the heavens, or in some cases history, with absolutes. Derrida wants to hollow out the space illicitly filled by metaphysics or at least to reinscribe metaphysical terms within language. What seems natural or essential turns out to be always already arbitrary, a function of the linguistic system that it claims to preexist, center, or ground.

According to Cavell, Derrida's deconstruction befits a French intellectual who understandably feels claustrophobic in a culture crammed with names like Leibniz, Kant, Schelling, and Heidegger (DT, 531). Cavell adds that if he lived in "a culture, call it France, the chief city of which had been producing world-historical literature, and which knew it, and fed the same samples of it to all the young who will occupy public positions, I would doubtless also be thinking of space as room and of some excavation or deconstruction in which to have my own thoughts" (DT, 531). For Derrida, then, "the land of thought is fully occupied as it were by the finished edifice of philosophy . . . so that room for thought must be made," say by deconstruction (MUW, 29–30). Trapped in a library, Derrida has to read his way out before writing. His work accordingly takes the form of prying open the seemingly airtight arguments that he studies.

As an American philosopher, Cavell feels as if he writes in a wilderness rather than in a long-finished building jammed with texts that he feels culturally obligated to get through. Cavell is not here debunking American culture but characterizing it, noting that in America "the question persists whether the land of thought has been discovered, and it is at best occupied by fragments, heaped in emergency, an anthology of rumor" (MUW, 30). Because "the first cabins of thought are still under construction" (MUW, 31), we (Americans) wonder "whether our voices, without echo, can make it to one another across the smallest fields"

(DT, 531). Again this isolation does not so much weaken American thought as define it: hence Cavell's respect not only for Thoreau and Emerson and the American movies discussed in *Pursuits* but also for the often-maligned first generation of American New Critics:

> I do not credit Heidegger with a better touch for litera-
> ture than [John Crowe] Ransom's, or Kenneth Burke's,
> or R. P. Blackmur's, or Paul Goodman's, but the Ameri-
> cans compose their theoretical works in a kind of scrip,
> good for exchange at the company store but worth next
> to nothing on the international market. It may seem a
> kind of private language. (To say of the New Critics
> that they composed their theory privately or locally
> seems to me truer than to say, as I hear it said, that
> they composed no theory, or little. And then one
> might look more fruitfully for the cause of what theory
> they produced.) (IQO, 205)

In his respect for the New Critics, Cavell underscores the value of critics' assuming the particular history of their place.

Whereas Derrida sees "metaphysics as coming to the wrong conclusions," Cavell, as an American philosopher, thus sees it "as coming to nothing at all," nothing, at any rate, philosophical (PAL, 12). Where Derrida sees in a meta-physics "a domineering construction" (UO, 13) and a "turn to excess or exaggeration" (MUW, 28), Cavell finds empti-ness, "a craving for nothingness," "a wish to exist outside language games—not so much as it were beyond language perhaps as before it" (MUW, 23). Metaphysics thus suggests emptiness to Cavell not only because it does not occupy or fill American thought but also because for him in metaphys-ics we desire to "empty out [our] contribution to words," so that something else beyond us—God, for example, nature, or even language itself—"exclusively takes over the respon-sibility for meaning" (WPC, 24).

As I have said, picturing metaphysics, or past philoso-phy, as a crowded space leads Derrida to search for its cracks and crevices. A seemingly solid, permanent, well-grounded, "natural" structure—metaphysics—ends up ap-pearing a hollow, makeshift, merely temporary contrivance uneasily suspended over an abyss. Picturing metaphysics as empty leads Cavell to think in terms of building, settling down, and inhabiting, like Thoreau in *Walden* or Wittgenstein in the *Philosophical Investigations* when he speaks of digging until the spade is turned (no. 217). Instead of denying Derrida's conclusion, say by reinstating metaphysics, he transvalues it. What Derrida stigmatizes as arbitrary (because not transcendentally or absolutely grounded) Cavell accepts as natural—improvised and otherwise dependent on human effort but not for that reason merely arbitrary or only conventional.

I say "only conventional" because in much contemporary literary theory, a dismissive "merely" or "only" precedes "conventional" as surely as winter leads to spring. Dismissed, again, are the claims of (merely) conventional categories to be ordinary, normal, objective, natural, rational, or essential. (I take this list from Fish's *Is There a Text in This Class?*) From this point of view, "natural," for example, is an irredeemably metaphysical term tainted, infected, or contaminated with the impurities that it tries to exclude.[5] These alleged impurities include contingency, repetition, accident, choice, and custom, among many others. In *Wittgenstein and Derrida*, one of the best recent accounts of deconstruction, Henry Staten sympathetically notes that from Derrida's point of view, "'repeatability,' as the condition for the existence of all idealities, whether they are the 'senses' or real or ideal objects, turns out to infect the entire domain of presence."[6] Similarly, echoing comments by de Man as well as by Derrida, Staten observes that in developing a "self" (still another metaphysical "ideality") we "fall" into a "perverse activity of invention, of fictionalization, *Erdichtung,*" and disintegration that leaves us with only "accidental transformations of related assemblages of inessentials."[7] In these deflating comments, Staten's Derrida is not so much bringing us down to earth as rubbing our noses in it, as in something unsavory.

Extending the reading of Thoreau described in my last chapter, Cavell uses contingency, variability, and temporality not to sully traditional philosophical categories but to humanize them. Derrida's demystification-with-a-vengeance gives way to an acceptance of human finitude and a probing that reaches bedrock in what we humans do (cf. *Philosophical Investigations,* no. 217). From Cavell's point of view, if repetition, fictionalization, and so on smell, they smell of mortality.

"Natural" accordingly remains a positive term in Cavell's thought, along with "necessary," "essential," "ordinary," and the others that Derrida debunks. He can speak, for instance, of the naturalness of ordinary language, of the deep sense of necessity that inheres in grammatical judgments (MWM, 92–93), even of "those necessities we cannot, being human, fail to know" (MWM, 96). He refuses, in other words, to let the "sheerly conventional" (TS, 40) subvert the natural. Although human ways of life differ, there is still a crucial difference between "poking at your food, perhaps with a fork, and pawing at it, or pecking at it" (WPC, 12). Some things are natural to us as humans, even essential.

Cavell realizes that his retention of terms like "natural" and "essential" leaves him open to the accusation of conservatism. As he puts it, "obeying nature is the perennial claim of the de Sades of history" (TS, 9), who have tried to make torture and repression seem natural and therefore inalterable. Although not often charged with sadism, ordinary-language philosophers have been accused of trying to stabilize usage by stigmatizing as "queer" or "ridiculous" (two of Austin and Wittgenstein's key terms of criticism) what clashes with their ideas of grammar and "normal" usage. In this crack at ordinary-language philosophy, "natural" ends up dignifying something resembling etiquette, where how to use words is on a par with how to set a table or use a fork. Cavell himself invites this charge by brazenly endorsing such quaint, Emily Post–sounding terms as sociability, gracefulness, honesty, dignity, practicality, and tact.

All of these values have been moralized or turned into rigid, seemingly metaphysical entities, with "tact," for instance, suggesting the ability not to mention something or touch upon it in certain social situations that can be identified once and for all. Cavell does not use "tact" this way. For him, much as gracefulness suggests "responsiveness, specificity of response to the unforeseen, say an improvisation of vision," tact connotes "touching [something] pertinently, fittingly, painfully if necessary" (BD, 21a–21b). He takes these definitions from a film, *Now Voyager*, which contests "the moralization of morality"—what I have called etiquette—by refusing to let it deprive us of good words like tact, gracefulness, and dignity.

Cavell's response to etiquette here parallels his response to metaphysics. Both etiquette and metaphysics freeze the very terms that he wants to reanimate. Well aware of the "surrealism" of what we call ordinary or natural, Cavell, like Thoreau, aims these words at a status quo that would reify them.[8] Instead of renouncing these terms or only begrudgingly using them, he reintroduces ideas that have admittedly become "tyrannical (e.g., existence, obligation, certainty, identity, reality, truth . . .) into the specific contexts in which they function naturally." "This is not a question of cutting big ideas down to size," or settling for a pared-down, makeshift, or "fallen" sense of "natural," "but of giving them the exact space in which they can move without corrupting" (MWM, 18). "Move" is a key word here: that space has to allow our everyday lives together to turn around and grow.

At first, then, it looks as if Cavell were trying to stop the free play of signification by appealing to how words are naturally or actually used. But the opposite is the case. "Naturally used" for him means creatively, diversely, flexibly. He wants to secure words not by metaphysically delimiting their meaning but by tying them to the flow of everyday life. In Cavell, again as in Thoreau and Wittgenstein,

> what we are asked to accept or suffer, in accepting forms of life as the given [or as the natural], is not, let us say, private property but separateness; not a particular fact of power but the fact that I am a man, therefore of *this* (range or scale of) capacity for work, for pleasure, for endurance, for appeal, for command, for understanding, for wish, for will, for teaching, for suffering. The precise range or scale is not knowable a priori, any more than the precise range or scale of a

word is to be known a priori. Of course you can *fix* the range; so can you bind a man or a woman, and not all the ways or senses of binding are knowable a priori. (WPC, 13–14)

But far from wishing to (further) bind men and women, Cavell wants to set them free. He is suggesting that we stand, or slump, "in need of something like transfiguration—some radical change, but as it were from inside, not by anything; . . . another birth, symbolizing a different order of natural reactions" (WPC, 14).

Using "natural" this dynamic way does not contradict Cavell's earlier emphasis on deciding things and taking responsibility but demands it. His reluctance to ground our judgments in "agreements expressible as decisions" partly stems from his feeling that we have not decided what we take for granted as natural, normal, philosophical, and so on. He wants us to have a say in defining these terms, a voice in our history. Arriving at what is ordinary and natural is thus an endless task, or as he puts it, the achievement of a life, where a human life is what we achieve.

An example from chapter 2 clarifies how the naturalness of ordinary language ensures our taking responsibility for what we say. In this example, a man stands up to stretch, grimacing in excruciating pain, then adds, perhaps urgently pointing to his breast, "There is *something* here accompanying my whine of pain" (CR, 337). Cavell suggests that the man's statement and gesture backfire: his "very words or rather the insistence with which in such an eventuality they are employed . . . exactly serve to break [the] natural connection [between sign and meaning]," making "the fact that an expression and what it expresses go together seem more or less accidental" (CR, 338). Cavell is not saying that a grimace or whine is natural in that an expression of pain has to take this form. We can imagine other ways of expressing pain, just as we can imagine other ways of eating, dressing, and so on. A grimace is natural, however, in being one way our culture expresses pain. The man in the example does not decide what counts as a grimace, a stretch, a gesture of emphasis, pointing, and so on. These categories not only preexist his actions, but define them (as desperate, insistent, and so forth). The man naturally raises his voice or thumps his breast to emphasize his point; he does not speak in a falsetto or rapidly make a circle with his left hand. These could count as signs of emphasis but in the way of life presumed by the story they do not. As indicators of emphasis, they would seem indecipherable, even ridiculous.

The man in the example does not invent what he hopes will count as a new form of expressing pain—a different whine, say, or an improved cry. He could try to do this but even here others would read him as inventing something, where "inventing something" would be a cultural category that the man had not invented. The man, then, does not start from scratch; he does not unilaterally or arbitrarily decide many things in Cavell's example but naturally does them.

If the man thus does not decide what will count as reinforcing his whine of pain, he does, however, decide to reinforce his cry. He is accordingly responsible for choosing to reinforce it. Maybe he understandably (or whimsically) distrusts his companions' concern for him or maybe he doubts his own sincerity. In any case, a grimace may be a natural expression of pain and still be misread (by suspicious observers) or misused (by someone feigning pain). Cavell is not eliminating choice here but insisting on its everyday importance. Contrasted to other signs we might invent, grimacing is a given, what we naturally do when we want to express pain. Contrasted to a physiological reflex or a wagging tail, grimacing is our choice. We do not have to be in pain to grimace. We even do not have to grimace to express pain. But we can.

Cavell here is typically trying to do justice to our separateness and our intimacy, our mutual attunement. As we have seen, he can use our mutual attunement to puncture the illusion of separateness, as when he suggests that Othello's intimacy with Desdemona belies and even brings about his stated uncertainty about her loyalty. And he can use our separateness to undermine the illusion of intimacy, as when he shows that Thoreau withdraws from his neighbors not to distance himself from them but to bring out the distance already there—the distance that their everyday activities veil. But intimacy and separateness finally come together in Cavell: each ends up requiring the other, much as I have said the naturalness of ordinary language demands our taking responsibility for what we say. Intimacy can foster separateness, as the couples in *Pursuits* show; acknowledging separateness is similarly crucial to intimacy. Human relationships consequently depend on choice, risk, and effort, but we choose to let ourselves be known, we risk acknowledging our expressions as us, and we struggle against our fear of exposure, of being found out.

The Sufficiency of Finitude

We can grimace (or whine, say "ouch," or whatever) to express pain: such a statement brings out Cavell's commitment to the obvious (the statement ought to sound trite), his appreciation of admittedly conventional signs and gestures (what we label a grimace and so on), and his affirmation of human intimacy, what he calls our mutual attunement (we can instantly signal our pain to someone else). What Cavell accepts in this example the literary theorists that I have been discussing find disappointing. These theorists for different reasons read "accepts" here as "puts up with" or "settles for," as we put up with a headache or settle for second place. From this point of view, signs, gestures, and literary works are too indirect, too problematic, too fleeting, too mediated, too superficial, and too imprecise to bridge the gap between us and others. Words themselves turn out to be desperate expedients, straws we latch onto as we nevertheless drown, fall, or otherwise lose our way.

This view of recent theory may seem unnecessarily bleak but I think that appearing to rise above what Cavell accepts here (even, or maybe especially, if human intimacy disappears as a result) is crucial to these theorists' sense of themselves. Facing up to our terminal separateness and uncertainty and not wishing them away as Cavell seems to do establishes these theorists as tough-minded, uncompromising, rigorous, and suspicious ("the hermeneutics of suspicion" being one popular label for recent theory). They see themselves as seeking a tighter connection with texts and other people than everyday life demands, as consequently staring harder at the text and otherwise paying closer attention to it than we ordinarily do. The often-stated dedication of these theorists to close, good, or slow reading is thus borne out by their facing up to the contamination of knowledge by language, the duplicity and violence of everyday relationships, the endlessness of interpretation, the baselessness of the self, the anguish of dispersion, the irony of repetition, and the disappointing equivocality and grim finitude of all human creations.

An influential critique of deconstruction that I have been criticizing throughout this book takes Derrida and de Man at their word.[9] Put very simply, this critique concedes that interpreting a text seems imprecise when contrasted to figuring out the answer to a problem in arithmetic. But while we cannot be absolutely certain about the meaning of a literary work (or a remark by a friend, a smile, and so on), we can be probably right, or sure enough. From this point of view, recent theorists (for some unexplained reason) expect too much. Their commitment to certainty is admirable, but out of place in literary criticism and everyday life, where as finite, limited creatures, we have to be content with half-truths, probabilities, inferences, educated guesses, and so on.

Cavell also speaks of the sufficiency of human finitude. But for him, instead of inexplicably expecting too much from human affairs, skepticism understandably recoils from their considerable power. In Cavell's account, the skeptic deprives himself of our ordinary links with the world and each other and then tries—unsuccessfully—to repair these links all by himself. "Deprives" suggests not that these connections are initially frayed but that if anything they can feel too tight. From Cavell's point of view, we may be not confined by words but all too exposed by them; not uncertain about others but too sure; not interested in change but afraid of it; not having to make others and the world present but having to acknowledge their presence. Intimacy may be our problem, avoidance our typical response, and exposure our ultimate fate.

I say "we" here and not "the skeptic" or "the deconstructionist" in order to indicate everyone's participation in the self-mystification that Cavell is describing. In the view of recent theory that I have taken here, reasons keep collapsing into excuses, epistemological or theoretical dilemmas into pretexts. This makes contemporary literary theory look less technical or specialized but more human. The feelings that I have been discussing in de Man and Derrida are not just in them but in us. These feelings are not so much problems requiring solutions as desires needing treatment, day in and day out, outside as well as inside the seminar.

NOTES

1. When I asked Cavell about this remark, he responded, "I had, with a few other philosophers, met Derrida in Paris in the summer of 1970, arranged by a group that included Herbert Dreyfus. . . . I was very impressed in the exchanges I had with Derrida those few days that summer, and we got along personally, I thought, notably well, ending on an almost familiar basis. He seemed to have read at least some of *Must We Mean . . . ?* (given him, I gathered, by Dreyfus) and gave me a collection of his books and monographs. I opened *L'écriture et la différence* on the plane back from Paris, and recognized in the opening paragraph that its use of French was intricate, allusive, playful, beyond my competence in the language. I tried again with a dictionary when I got home, but it was still no use. My reference to him in the Preface to *The Senses of Walden* was prompted immediately by Geoffrey Hartman's asking me (after hearing the version of my opening chapter of *Senses* that I read as my first Gauss Seminar in February, 1971) whether I knew anything of Derrida. I told him what I just told you; he was not surprised. My embarrassed remark in the Preface about my insufficient knowledge of the French is really based on hardly more than a set of radio interviews of Lévi-Strauss I came across (in French), which is where I got my first taste of how extensive a new French network, beyond my ken, had become (my ken pretty well ending, at that time, with Sartre, Camus, Merleau-Ponty, and Bachelard). I did not even know that Derrida and Lévi-Strauss were in disagreement on the question of writing" (January 8, 1985, letter).

2. Some notable exceptions include Jay Cantor, "On Stanley Cavell," *Raritan* 1 (Summer 1981): 48–67; John Hollander, "Stanley Cavell and *The Claim of Reason*," *Critical Inquiry* 6 (Summer 1980): 575–88; Stanley Bates's essay-review of *The Claim of Reason*, in *Philosophy and Literature* 4 (Spring 1980): 266–73; Robert Mankin, "An Introduction to *The Claim of Reason*," *Salmagundi* 67 (Summer 1985): 66–89; Richard Eldridge, "Philosophy and the Achievement of

Community: Rorty, Cavell and Criticism," *Metaphilosophy* 14 (April 1983): 107–25; Arnold Davidson, "The Spirit in Which Things Are Said," *London Review of Books* 6 (December 20, 1984–January 24, 1985): 17–18; Timothy Gould, "Stanley Cavell and the Plight of the Ordinary," in *Images in Our Souls: Cavell, Psychoanalysis, and Cinema*, ed. Joseph H. Smith and William Kerrigan (Baltimore: Johns Hopkins University Press, 1987), pp. 109–36; and Karen Hanson, "Being Doubted, Being Assured," in ibid., pp. 187–201. My account of Cavell owes something to all of these pioneering essays as well as to others cited below.

3. Geoffrey Hartman, *Criticism in the Wilderness* (New Haven: Yale University Press, 1980), p. 242, n. 10. In "The Culture of Criticism," *PMLA* 99 (May 1984), Hartman similarly points out, "It was not until Stanley Cavell's *The Senses of Walden* (1972) that philosophy brought 'texture' to literary studies and perhaps—if we add Cavell's writings on the movies—to our perception of what the American is in terms of cultural density rather than cultural humility" (p. 393, n. 15).

4. In a review of *Pursuits of Happiness*, Michael Wood observes of *The Claim of Reason*, "The writing is remarkable here, the philosopher as novelist gives density of detail to fleshless old questions" ("One Mo' Time," *New York Review of Books*, January 21, 1982, p. 29). In praising Cavell's "elliptically parabolic method" in *The Claim of Reason*, Hollander similarly points out that Cavell's "anecdotes, scenarios, little parables, and exemplary stories are better than those of most novelists" ("Stanley Cavell and *The Claim of Reason*," p. 582). Finally, finding in Cavell's work "a new kind of storytelling," Cantor concludes, "It isn't a novel, yet it is like a novel (what is a novel like?): a murmurous undertone of the novel's work, its constant accompaniment and encouragement, like Kafka's prayer" ("On Stanley Cavell," pp. 66–67).

5. Wood, "One Mo' Time," p. 29. In keeping with Cavell's own emphasis on speech and conversation, Wood reports, "I shall live happily for some time with the sound of *The Claim of Reason*" (ibid.). In a July 22, 1977, *Times Literary Supplement* review of *Must We Mean What We Say?* F. E. Sparshott offers a much less flattering description of Cavell's distinctive voice, calling it "powerful and individual but above all insistent" and finally "overcharged" and "garrulous."

6. See Anthony Kenny's review of *The Claim of Reason*, "Clouds of Not Knowing," *Times Literary Supplement*, April 18, 1980, p. 449 (Kenny faults Cavell's "self-indulgent" style, especially its penchant for apparently gratuitous distinctions, qualifications, and parenthetical interruptions). Mary Mothersill's comment occurs in

her review of three Cavell books in *Journal of Philosophy* 72 (January 30, 1975): 33 (she, too, adds that "the confessional mode invites self-indulgence," to which Cavell succumbs). For other criticisms of Cavell, see Anthony Palmer's review of *The Claim of Reason*, in *Mind* (April 1982): 293 (Palmer also laments Cavell's "self-indulgence," which is "proportional to the length and number of parenthetical remarks"); M. Glouberman's review of *Must We Mean What We Say?* in *Review of Metaphysics* 32 (June 1979): 913 (Glouberman simply calls Cavell's style "inexcusable"); and the Sparshott review cited in n. 5 ("Cavell fills his sentences with parentheses and his paragraphs with qualifications," but "the qualifications do not refine but cancel. The reader feels not that his life is being restored, but that Cavell is hiding"). Even the otherwise sympathetic Arthur C. Danto, in "Philosophy and/as Film and/as if Philosophy," *October* 23 (Winter 1982): 13, objects that Cavell writes "at times like an angel and at times like Woody Woodpecker." For the accusation of anti-intellectualism, see especially Vincent Hope's review of *The Claim of Reason*, "Scepticism as Tragedy," *Inquiry* 24 (December 1981): 470–80, where Hope charges that Cavell abandons "reason for imagination, arguments for images" (p. 470) and "revels in the philosophical fairy-tale" (p. 471).

7. Danto, "Philosophy and/as Film and/as if Philosophy," pp. 13–14. On love, or at least intimacy, as a response courted by Romantic literature, see Morris Eaves, *William Blake's Theory of Art* (Princeton: Princeton University Press, 1982), chap. 4.

8. Paul de Man, *The Rhetoric of Romanticism* (New York: Columbia University Press, 1984), pp. 286–87.

9. I borrow this description of Cavell's achievement from Davidson, "The Spirit in Which Things Are Said," p. 18.

10. See my *Does Deconstruction Make Any Difference?* (Bloomington: Indiana University Press, 1985), p. 36.

11. (Ithaca: Cornell University Press, 1982).

12. For a fuller discussion of Goodheart's book, *The Skeptic Disposition in Contemporary Criticism* (Princeton: Princeton University Press, 1984), see my review, "Criticizing Deconstruction," *Salmagundi* 72 (Fall 1986): 267–71. I should add that I am also not the first to want to apply Cavell to the debate surrounding deconstruction. In addition to Cantor, "On Stanley Cavell," see Richard Rorty, *The Consequences of Pragmatism* (Minneapolis: University of Minnesota Press, 1982), especially p. 76, where Rorty goes so far as to call Cavell an admirer of Derrida, a remark that captures only half the picture that I want to sketch here. Stephen Melville similarly brings to light Cavell's similarities to Derrida while slighting their differences in "The Situation of Writing," *Chicago Review* 29 (Autumn

1977): 103–16. See also Melville's *Philosophy beside Itself* (Minneapolis: University of Minnesota Press, 1986), especially pp. 18–23, 142–56.

13. Cantor, "On Stanley Cavell," pp. 50–51.

14. Charles Altieri, *Act and Quality* (Amherst: University of Massachusetts Press, 1981), p. 27; and M. H. Abrams, "Construing and Deconstructing," in *Romanticism and Contemporary Criticism*, ed. Morris Eaves and Michael Fischer (Ithaca: Cornell University Press, 1986), p. 130. On Hume and Derrida, see also Denis Dutton's "Why Intentionalism Won't Go Away," in *Literature and the Question of Philosophy*, ed. Anthony J. Cascardi (Baltimore: Johns Hopkins University Press, 1987), where Dutton remarks that "just as Hume's critique of causality did not prevent him from playing billiards, . . . Derrida's deconstruction of presence does not keep him from being absent from, present at, or sleeping through seminars" (p. 208). Two other typical references to deconstruction and skepticism are worth mentioning here. Commenting on the novel and history, Robert Alter cites "the radical epistemological skepticism of much current literary theory" ("The Novel and the Sense of the Past," *Salmagundi* 68–69 [Fall 1985-Winter 1986]: 103). And in *Philosophy of the Literary Symbolic* (Tallahassee: Florida State University Press, 1983), Hazard Adams makes much of "the skepticism of deconstruction" (p. 199).

15. *Deconstruction Theory and Practice* (London and New York: Methuen, 1982), p. xii.

16. 3d ed., trans. G. E. M. Anscombe (New York: Macmillan, 1968).

17. See Altieri, *Act and Quality*, pp. 23–52. For comparable appeals to Wittgenstein, see Cantor, "On Stanley Cavell," pp. 66–67; M. H. Abrams, "How to Do Things with Texts," *Partisan Review* 46 (1979): 570–71; and James Guetti, "Wittgenstein and Literary Theory," *Raritan* 4 (1984): 72–79. On Cavell's differences from these critics, see my "Stanley Cavell's Wittgenstein," in *Literary Theory between Philosophies*, ed. Reed Way Dasenbrock (Minneapolis: University of Minnesota Press, forthcoming).

18. Christopher Norris, *The Deconstructive Turn* (London and New York: Methuen, 1983), p. 35.

CHAPTER TWO

1. Jacques Derrida, "Force and Signification," in *Writing and Difference*, trans. Alan Bass (Chicago: University of Chicago Press, 1978), p. 6.

2. For this way of putting it, see Paul de Man, "Shelley Disfig-

ured," in *Deconstruction and Criticism*, Harold Bloom et al. (New York: Seabury Press, 1979), pp. 39–41, 68–69. For a similar figure, see J. Hillis Miller, *The Linguistic Moment* (Princeton: Princeton University Press, 1985), where he remarks that a poem by Wallace Stevens "hollows Emerson and Whitman out, gives their key figures one final twist that shatters the structure based on them and shows it to have been baseless" (p. 413). Cited in text as LM.

3. On the lingering influence of the New Criticism, see William E. Cain, *The Crisis in Criticism* (Baltimore: Johns Hopkins University Press, 1984).

4. I have taken this comparison—and the ones that follow—from Cleanth Brooks's important chapter, "The Heresy of Paraphrase," in *The Well Wrought Urn* (New York: Harvest Books, 1947).

5. "Pure and Impure Poetry" (1943), in *Critical Theory since Plato*, ed. Hazard Adams (New York: Harcourt Brace Jovanovich, 1971), p. 992.

6. *The Languages of Criticism and the Structure of Poetry* (Toronto: University of Toronto Press, 1953), p. 184.

7. "Objective Interpretation" (1960), in *Validity in Interpretation* (New Haven: Yale University Press, 1967), pp. 216, 218, 210. For a similar point, see also p. 216.

8. Ibid., pp. 217–18.

9. *Anatomy of Criticism* (Princeton: Princeton University Press, 1957), pp. 77–78.

10. "Force and Signification," pp. 6, 5. For a similar use of the word "soliciting," see Derrida's "Differance," in *Margins of Philosophy*, trans. Alan Bass (Chicago: University of Chicago Press, 1982), p. 21.

11. *Blindness and Insight* (1971; reprint, Minneapolis: University of Minnesota Press, 1983), p. 26. Cited in text as BI.

12. In *Day of the Leopards* (New Haven: Yale University Press, 1976).

13. (Cambridge: Harvard University Press, 1980).

14. Derrida, "Force and Signification," p. 14.

15. Ibid., p. 24.

16. Most of Hirsch's metaphors for meaning work this way. In discussing unconscious meanings, for instance, he compares the text to an iceberg: "the larger part may be submerged, but the submerged part has to be connected with [and can be inferred from] the part that is exposed" (*Validity in Interpretation*, p. 53). For a deconstructive critique of this tendency in Hirsch, see Henry Staten, *Wittgenstein and Derrida* (Lincoln: University of Nebraska Press, 1984), pp. 142–45.

17. "Structure, Sign, and Play in the Discourse of the Human

Sciences," in *Writing and Difference*, p. 292. "Not to worry" is Fish's often-quoted phrase, from *Is There a Text in This Class?* p. 321.

18. *Fiction and Repetition* (Cambridge: Harvard University Press, 1982), p. 25.

19. Miller, *Linguistic Moment*, p. 177. Earlier, commenting on *The Triumph of Life*, Miller remarks that "each new scene gives the elements of the poem another twist, making [the reader] forget what had come before, masking it. . . . The reader cannot even clearly hold in his mind all at once the intricate sequence of permutations making up the poem as we have it" (p. 151). Each shape that the reader proposes for this poem (or for any poem) is consequently "no more than a frail spider web over a rushing stream" (p. 331). Along similar lines, throughout *Is There a Text in This Class?* Fish registers his opposition to "the assumption that there *is* a sense, that it is embedded or encoded in the text, and that it can be taken in at a single glance. These assumptions are, in order, positivist, holistic, and spatial" (p. 158).

20. Hirsch, "Objective Interpretation," p. 214.

21. Fish, *Is There a Text in This Class?* p. 315.

22. In "The Politics of Interpretation," Cavell similarly objects that "Austin was intent on preventing such a [skeptical] story from getting off the ground," a desire that Cavell regards as "a grave limitation in his philosophizing—a refusal, in effect, to consider why it looked as if he were defending common beliefs" (TS, 33). See also "The Division of Talent," in *Themes out of School*, pp. 534–35. In going on to say that a goldfinch (Austin's example) does not count as a generic object in this context, Cavell is using "generic object" not to suggest that "there are two kinds of objects in the world, but rather to summarize the spirit in which an object is under discussion, the kind of problem that has arisen about it, the problem in which it presents itself as the focus of investigation" (CR, 52–53).

23. "Error in Paul de Man," in *The Yale Critics: Deconstruction in America*, ed. Jonathan Arac, Wlad Godzich, and Wallace Martin (Minneapolis: University of Minnesota Press, 1983), p. 102. I would argue that such a canonical text or passage counts as the poststructuralist's "provisional object of knowledge," to borrow a phrase from A. J. Cascardi's "Skepticism and Deconstruction," *Philosophy and Literature* 8 (April 1984): 3. Cascardi goes on to say that the deconstructionist's "predicament is not uncertainty but radical indeterminacy" (ibid.), a distinction that eludes me. Cascardi's article is a sophisticated demonstration of some of the differences between deconstruction and some forms of epistemological skepti-

cism. In my view, however, these differences are offset by the similarities between deconstruction and the skeptical recital that I present here.

24. I would add that the generic object itself is similarly a historical product. Marking it brings to light that it is already marked—by being made or bought, for example, and placed in the study. The philosopher prefers not to notice these facts—the success of the skeptical project may depend on their suppression—which is a way of saying that the skeptic abstracts the generic object as well as himself from history. Following the early Marx, I would go so far as to say that the philosopher also removes the senses themselves from history. See Marx's "Private Property and Communism," where he concludes that the *"forming* of the five senses is a labor of the entire history of the world down to the present" (*The Economic and Philosophic Manuscripts of 1844*, ed. Dirk J. Struick [New York: International Publishers, 1964], p. 141). For an astute commentary on this point in Marx, see Fredric Jameson, *The Political Unconscious* (Ithaca: Cornell University Press, 1981), pp. 62–63, 229–33. In "Wallace Stevens," *New Orleans Review* 11 (Spring 1984), Jameson calls Stevens's poetic practice "rigorously epistemological in all the worst senses of this word. In Stevens we never have anything but an abstract subject contemplating an object world which is thereby construed as being equally abstract. As with the great 'illustrations' of classical epistemology (in professional philosophy), where impoverished tokens from the external world (a desk, say) are drawn in as sheer indifferent 'examples,' the items of the external world must in Stevens equally be laundered of their cultural and social semantics, just as the social world and the existence of other people must equally be bracketed" (p. 12). Though much more sympathetic to traditional epistemology, Cavell does speak of "the senses" in skepticism as "an invention, a production of dialectic, an historical-philosophical construction" (CR, 224).

25. In *Must We Mean What We Say?* Cavell argues that "the philosopher is no more magically equipped to remove a question from its natural environment than he is to remove himself from any of the conditions of intelligible discourse. Or rather, he may remove himself, but his mind will not follow" (MWM, 41). It seems to me equally true that while the philosopher may try to remove his mind, his body will not follow.

26. Fish, *Is There a Text in This Class?* p. 346.

27. Fish's example from Blake also works this way. Here, though, instead of producing additional evidence, Fish appeals to the already established view of Blake—the very view that he wants

to unsettle: "Here the task [of coming up with a reading of "The Tyger" as a gastrointestinal allegory] is easy because according to the critical consensus there is no belief so bizarre that Blake could not have been committed to it and it would be no trick at all to find some elaborate system of alimentary significances (Pythagorean? Swedenborgian? Cabbalist?) which he could be presumed to have known" (ibid., p. 348). By calling on received scholarly opinion about Blake and even advising those readers who doubt the plausibility of his reading "to consult some recent numbers of *Blake Studies*" (p. 349), Fish is again playing the game that he wants to question. Apparently, as he himself says, it is "the only game in town" (p. 355).

28. "From Restricted to General Economy: A Hegelianism without Reserve," in *Writing and Difference*, p. 260.

29. "Construing and Deconstructing," pp. 173, 170.

Chapter Three

1. Samuel Taylor Coleridge, "Mechanic and Organic Form," in *English Romantic Writers*, ed. David Perkins (New York: Harcourt, Brace & World, 1967), p. 500.

2. "The Critic, the Public, the Past," *Salmagundi* 68–69 (Fall 1985–Winter 1986): 218.

3. "Pluralism in the Classroom," *Critical Inquiry* 12 (Spring 1986): 475.

4. "Poetry for Poetry's Sake," in Adams, *Critical Theory since Plato*, p. 741. On the text as body—and the body as text—see also James K. Mishlalani, "Kafka: Text's Body, Body's Text," *Philosophy and Literature* 10 (April 1986): 56–64. In case my references to Barzun and Bradley seem out of date, here is Jerome J. McGann in *The Romantic Ideology* (Chicago: University of Chicago Press, 1983) referring to the "heart of the poem" (p. 13) and objecting to "reducing poetic works to a network of related themes and ideas—a condition of being which no artistic product can tolerate without loss of its soul" (p. 11).

5. Murray Krieger, "Mediation, Language, and Vision in the Reading of Literature," in Adams, *Critical Theory since Plato*, pp. 1235, 1233. Subsequent references are to page number and are inserted in the text.

6. Georges Poulet, "Criticism and the Experience of Interiority," in *The Structuralist Controversy*, ed. Richard Macksey and Eugenio Donato (Baltimore: Johns Hopkins University Press,

1972), p. 57. Subsequent references are to page number and are inserted in the text.

7. "Geneva or Paris? The Recent Work of Georges Poulet," *University of Toronto Quarterly* 39 (April 1970): 221.

8. "The Critic as Host," in Bloom et al., *Deconstruction and Criticism*, pp. 246–47.

9. On the importance of these essays to de Man's work as a whole, see Tilottama Rajan, "Displacing Post-Structuralism: Romantic Studies after Paul de Man," *Studies in Romanticism* 24 (Winter 1985): 451–74. In Stanley Corngold's words, "The continuities [between de Man's early and late essays] tend to show de Man to an extraordinary degree the captive of his beginnings" ("Error in Paul de Man," p. 92).

10. *Speech and Phenomena*, trans. David B. Allison (Evanston: Northwestern University Press, 1973); "Signature Event Context," in *Margins of Philosophy*.

11. *Of Grammatology*, trans. Gayatri Chakravorty Spivak (Baltimore: Johns Hopkins University Press, 1976), p. 240. Cited in text as OG.

12. Derrida takes up what he sees as Austin's similar uneasiness with utterances recited on stage in "Signature Event Context," in *Margins of Philosophy*, pp. 324ff.

13. Along similar lines, Derrida cautions us in *Of Grammatology* that "one cannot abstract from the written text to rush to the signified it *would* mean, since the signified is here the text itself. It is so little a matter of looking for a *truth signified* by these writings (metaphysical or psychological truth: Jean Jacques's life behind his work) that if the texts that interest us *mean* something, it is the engagement and the appurtenance that encompass existence and writing in the same *tissue*, the same *text*" (p. 150).

14. See also *Of Grammatology*, p. 158, where Derrida notes that "the writer writes *in* a language and *in* a logic whose proper system, laws, and life his discourse by definition cannot dominate absolutely. He uses them only by letting himself, after a fashion and up to a point, be governed by the system. And the reading must always aim at a certain relationship, unperceived by the writer, between what he commands and what he does not command of the patterns of the language that he uses."

15. In his discussion of Plato in *Dissemination*, trans. Barbara Johnson (Chicago: University of Chicago Press, 1981), Derrida introduces much the same metaphor: "Writing would indeed be the signifier's capacity to repeat itself by itself, mechanically, without a

living soul to sustain or attend it in its repetition, that is to say, without truth's *presenting itself* anywhere" (p. 111).

16. One of Cavell's strongest statements on the necessity that resides in criteria occurs in *Must We Mean What We Say?*: "It is a wonderful step towards understanding the abutment of language and the world when we see it to be a matter of convention. But this idea, like every other, endangers as it releases the imagination. For some will then suppose that a private meaning is not more arbitrary than one arrived at publicly, and that since language inevitably changes, there is no reason not to change it arbitrarily. Here we need to remind ourselves that ordinary language is natural language, and that its changing is natural" (MWM, 42).

17. Cavell links Wittgenstein's concentration on pain in the *Philosophical Investigations* to the fascination of psychoanalysis and cinema with the sufferings of women. By the turn of the century, "psychic reality, the fact of the existence of mind, has become believable primarily in its feminine (you may say passive) aspect" (MUW, 15).

18. As Cavell adds in *The Claim of Reason*, "I want my existence proven by evidence that I cannot supply, and need not. And the same goes for the existence of others" (CR, 471).

19. Reading others takes an important turn in the work of Annette Kolodny, Susan Gubar, and other feminist critics interested in showing that the interpretive strategies we apply to other people as well as to texts are historically conditioned and therefore "gender-inflected." See Kolodny's "A Map for Rereading: Gender and the Interpretation of Literary Texts" and Susan Gubar, "'The Blank Page' and the Issues of Female Creativity," in *The New Feminist Criticism,* ed. Elaine Showalter (New York: Pantheon Books, 1985), pp. 46–62 and 292–313. Naomi Scheman's unpublished essay "Othello's Doubt/Desdemona's Death: The Engendering of Scepticism'" extends this line of thought to classical skepticism. Along similar lines, toward the end of *The Claim of Reason* Cavell speculates that knowledge of others "will be eroticized, enacted in forms of sexual life" (CR, 470) (he mentions sadism and masochism, connecting them with the wish for "absolute recognition of and by another" [CR, 470].) On skepticism as a male project, see above, pp. 31–32.

20. I take these possibilities from "Knowing and Acknowledging," in *Must We Mean What We Say?* p. 264.

21. On Keaton and Chaplin, see *Themes out of School,* pp. 175–76.

22. On the different roles played by the outsider in other-minds and external-world skepticism, see *The Claim of Reason*, pp. 416–18.

23. "Geneva or Paris?" p. 221.

24. This statement occurs in de Man's review of Nathalie Sarraute's *L'Ere du soupçon*, in *Monde nouveau* 11 (1956): 59. Quoted in Corngold, "Error in Paul de Man," p. 106, n. 4.

CHAPTER FOUR

1. I take this way of putting it from "Hamlet's Burden of Proof," where Cavell concludes that "Shakespeare's dramas, like Freud's, thus propose our coming to know what we cannot just not know; like philosophy" (DK, 191). For a similar way of making this point, see Cavell's "Recounting Gains, Showing Losses: Reading *The Winter's Tale*," which describes a working mind, "a mind still in command of language," as one "that cannot simply not count" but must "miscount, or discount, to misattribute, the thing it finds to be unbearable to count" (DK, 209).

2. On this relationship between philosophical skepticism and literature, see also "Hamlet's Burden of Proof," where Cavell says: "The burden of my story in spinning the interplay of philosophy with literature is not that of applying philosophy to literature, where so-called literary works would become kinds of illustrations of matters already independently known. It would better express my refrain to say that I take the works I am drawn to read out loud in public (beginning with those . . . of Shakespeare) as studies of matters that your philosophy has (unassessably, left to itself) intellectualized as skepticism, whether in Descartes's or Hume's or Kant's pictures of that inescapably, essentially, human possibility" (DK, 179). Asked about his persistent reliance on literature, Cavell similarly notes that "I'm looking in these texts not for illustrations, but for allegories, experiments, conceptual investigations, a working out of this complex of issues, and I claim that that is what they are, that's what produces these texts" (IQO, 229–30). See also p. 234 of this same essay, where Cavell notes that he wants literary texts (in this case Romantic ones) "not just to illustrate a prior philosophical problem of skepticism, but themselves to be interpretations of the same problem, to be as ground-floor, if that's the right metaphor, as philosophy itself."

3. On parents' figuratively eating the children whom they fail to acknowledge, see also "On Makavejev on Bergman," in *Themes out of School*, p. 129.

4. Along similar lines, Cavell notes that "what is to be acknowledged is always something specifically done or not done; the exact instance of my denial of you" (WV, 128). "It will not count as an acknowledgment of your being late for you to register your knowledge that there is tardiness in the world; nor will it count if you register your knowledge to the company you are leaving rather than to the company you have kept waiting" (WV, 226).

5. In "More of *The World Viewed*," Cavell calls movies "inherently anarchic" because their "unappeasable appetite for stories of love is for stories in which love, to be found, must find its own community, apart from, but with luck still within, society at large; an enclave within it; stories in which society as a whole, and its laws, can no longer provide or deny love" (WV, 214).

6. In *The Claim of Reason*, Cavell pictures the intertwining of comedy with tragedy this way: "The idea of the natural here [celebrated by comedy] is not at odds with, but rather meets, the idea of the sociable. This meeting of the natural and the sociable is something comic writers preach, knowing also, something that writers of tragedy see, that the human being is apt, is fit, to be neither" (CR, 415–16).

7. Silencing the heroine in these films, depriving her of a voice in her history, fits in with Elaine Showalter's more general description of women as constituting a "muted group." See Showalter's "Feminist Criticism in the Wilderness," in Showalter, *The New Feminist Criticism*, pp. 243–70.

8. Cavell's interest in claiming a therapeutic function for Wittgenstein's writing accordingly leads him to say of Wittgenstein what I am suggesting about these comedies: "Irony is as much [Wittgenstein's] enemy as his aspiration. . . . The laughter he used in philosophical diagnosis is more good-humored than it is in the spirit of irony; perhaps more sociable, and certainly more self-catching" (TS, 196). On sociability, see above, p. 89.

9. It follows that the refusal to be nourished suggests "something between a fear of being polluted or poisoned, a terror of trusting, and a wish not to have a body" (TS, 135) (Cavell is discussing the woman in Antonioni's *Red Desert*). Attitudes toward food and the body also figure prominently in Cavell's essay on *Coriolanus*, "*Coriolanus* and Interpretations of Politics," reprinted in *Themes out of School*.

10. Elsewhere, especially in *The World Viewed* and "What Photography Calls Thinking," Cavell speaks of a text's (or film's) "self-acknowledgment." See *The World Viewed*, p. 123, and "What Photography Calls Thinking," p. 3. I am more interested here,

however, in the reader's relationship with the text than in the text's self-consciousness.

11. Still another question raised by Cavell's reading might be put as follows: how can he stop theorizing about his data when, as he himself admits, only a theory "can tell you what to look for, or what counts, as evidence" (WV, 192)? Cavell does not directly answer this question, obviously an important one in recent theory, especially in the work of Fish.

12. For Cavell, theatricalizing others is not just a hypothetical possibility but in contemporary culture a fact of everyday experience that the news, for example, reinforces. He concludes the *King Lear* essay by describing the present as

> an age in which the organs of news, in the very totality and talent of their coverage, become distractions from what is happening, presenting everything happening as overwhelmingly present, like events in old theater. . . . We [consequently] no longer know what is and is not news, what is and is not a significant fact of our present history, what is and is not relevant to one's life. The newspaper tells me that everything is relevant, but I cannot really accept that because it would mean that I do not have one life, to which some things are relevant and some not. I cannot really deny it either because I do not know why things happen as they do and why I am not responsible for any or all of it. And so to the extent that I still have feeling to contend with, it is a generalized guilt, which only confirms my paralysis; or else I convert the disasters and sensations reported to me into topics of conversation, for mutual entertainment, which in turn irritates the guilt. (MWM, 348)

One function of tragedy today, Cavell goes on to say, "would be to show me that this view of the world is itself chosen, and theatrical" (MWM, 348)—that we can either "continue to aestheticize the world, put that form of distance between it and our experience of it, say by converting all our experience into a mode of viewing" or we can "learn to taste again, so that we can learn to maintain our disgust more easily than we learn to maintain what disgusts us" (TS, 137). On acting and the presentation of the news on television, see also "The Fact of Television," in *Themes out of School*, p. 256. On tasting, see above, n. 9.

13. In "What Photography Calls Thinking," Cavell similarly links the text's self-acknowledgment to "its knowledge of others, of *me*" (p. 3).

14. On structuralism as a way of "making the text interesting, of combating the boredom which lurks behind every work," see

Jonathan Culler, *Structuralist Poetics* (Ithaca: Cornell University Press), pp. 262–63.

15. Pp. 91, 102, 104.

16. Wlad Godzich, "The Domestication of Derrida," in Arac, Godzich, and Martin, *The Yale Critics: Deconstruction in America*, p. 25.

17. I advance a version of this argument in *Does Deconstruction Make Any Difference?* especially in chap. 3.

CHAPTER FIVE

1. More exactly, Howarth notes that *The Senses of Walden* has gained the reputation of producing "the first deconstructive reading of an American classic." While Howarth does not explicitly endorse this judgment, he also never repudiates it. Instead he suggests that Cavell resembles M. H. Abrams, Northrop Frye, and other predeconstructive critics "only slightly," adding that "he clearly does not seek to reconstruct *Walden*" ("On Reading *Walden*," *Thoreau Quarterly* 14 [Summer/Fall 1982]: 133). Howarth's essay appears in a special issue of *Thoreau Quarterly* dedicated to *The Senses of Walden*, called by the editors "the most searching critical study of *Walden* ever written." In this same issue see Karen Hanson, "Sounding the Philosophic Voice," and Frederick Garber, "Thoreau's Ladder of Alertness," useful summaries of Cavell's approach to writing in *Walden*.

2. Derrida, *Of Grammatology*, p. 136. My account of Derrida here focuses on only one moment—the deconstruction of the speech-writing distinction—in his complex writings.

3. Pp. 569, 570.

4. Ibid., p. 570.

5. Ibid., p. 575.

6. "The Deconstructive Angel," *Critical Inquiry* 3 (Spring 1977): 427, 429.

7. Ibid., p. 437.

8. Ibid.

9. Ibid., p. 438.

10. Having pointed out a couple of times some possible similarities between Derrida and Hume, I should add that whereas Hume welcomes the disappearance of his doubts, Derrida resists it or at least fails to greet it with the enthusiasm that Hume displays when he writes in a famous passage, "I dine, I play a game of backgammon, I converse, and am merry with my friends; and when, after three or four hours' amusement, I would return to these speculations, they appear so cold, and strained, and ridicu-

lous, that I cannot find in my heart to enter them any further. Here, then, I find myself absolutely and necessarily determined to live, and talk, and act, like other people in the common affairs of life" (*A Treatise of Human Nature*, bk. I, pt. IV, sec. VII). In *Does Deconstruction Make Any Difference?* I argue that deconstruction, by contrast, results in begrudging attachment to the very conventions that the deconstructionist wishes to question.

11. I have in mind here Abrams's suggestion that "[Derrida] agrees that language works, then asks, 'But is it possible that it really works?' He concludes that, lacking an ultimate ground, it is absolutely not possible that it works, hence its working is only a seeming—that, in short, though texts may be legible, they are not intelligible, or determinately significant" ("How to Do Things with Texts," p. 571).

12. *On Certainty*, ed. G. E. M. Anscombe and G. H. von Wright (1969; reprint, New York: Harper Torchbooks, 1972), nos. 487, 498.

13. Blake's allegiance to writing deserves comparison with Thoreau's. Both men write not to diffuse presence but to establish it. On Blake's commitment to writing, see W. J. T. Mitchell, "Visible Language: Blake's Wond'rous Art of Writing," in Eaves and Fischer, *Romanticism and Contemporary Criticism*, pp. 46–86.

14. I take this example from Mitchell's already noted essay on Blake (see n. 13). On Wordsworth's uneasiness with writing, see Miller's reading of *The Prelude*, discussed in chap. 3.

15. Unpublished paper.

16. Commenting on Romanticism in *The Claim of Reason*, Cavell similarly makes isolation a means to intimacy and, eventually, community: "Human beings do not naturally desire isolation and incomprehension, but union or reunion, call it community. It is in faithfulness to that desire that one declares oneself unknown. . . . The wish to be extraordinary, exceptional, unique"—to stand up, or, in Thoreau's case, to stand out by placing himself "one mile from any neighbor" (SW, 11)—"thus reveals the wish to be ordinary, everyday. . . . So both the wish for the exceptional and for the everyday are foci of romanticism. One can think of romanticism as the discovery that the everyday is an exceptional achievement. Call it the achievement of the human" (CR, 463).

17. Cavell finds a comparable metaphorical investment in economic terms in *The Winter's Tale*. See "Recounting Gains, Showing Losses: Reading *The Winter's Tale*," in *Disowning Knowledge*, pp. 200–201.

18. Emerson, as Cavell reads him, makes a similar point when he identifies language with fate but goes on to argue that "intellect annuls Fate. So far as a man thinks, he is free," thereby granting

us "a say in what we mean," a voice in our history. See Cavell, "Genteel Responses to Kant? In Emerson's 'Fate' and in Coleridge's *Biographia Literaria*," pp. 49–50. In "Shelley Disfigured," de Man starts out with a similar view of language, only to reach a much more pessimistic conclusion not only about thought and individual existence but also about history. I discuss this essay at length in *Does Deconstruction Make Any Difference?* chap. 4.

19. Thoreau's salvaging "practical" here illustrates Cavell's more general point that "for the word to return, what is necessary is not that we compute complexities around it, and also not exactly that we surround it with simplicities, but that we see the complexities *it* has and the simplicity it may have on a given occasion if we let it" (SW, 63).

20. On Wittgenstein's bringing words back and his consequent penchant for wordplay, see "Existentialism and Analytical Philosophy," in *Themes out of School*, p. 231.

21. *Rhetoric of Romanticism*, pp. 70–71.

22. The posture we assume in reading partly explains Thoreau's remark that "a man sits as many risks as he runs" (SW, 49). On standing, sitting, and posture in Emerson and Thoreau, see Cavell, "Being Odd, Getting Even," pp. 106–8, and idem, "In Quest of the Ordinary," p. 237.

23. In part Thoreau leaves us in order to get us to move, thus illustrating Cavell's comment that "the faith of this romanticism, overcoming the old, is that we can still be moved to move, that we are free, if we will, to step upon our transport, that nature's absence—or its presence merely to sentiment or mood—is only the history of our turnings from it, in distraction or denial, through history or industry, with words or works" (WV, 114).

24. Thoreau's aspirations here anticipate Cavell's comment on some modernist paintings: "These works exist as abstracts of intimacy—declaring our common capacity and need for presentness, for clear separateness and singleness and connection [genuine connection hinging on acknowledging our separateness], for horizons and uprightness [cf. standing up, or out, in n. 16] and frontedness, for the simultaneity of a world, for openness and resolution" (WV, 118).

25. All of these writers, Cavell included, accordingly aim at arousing us from our self-stupefaction and getting us interested in our own lives, a goal also pursued (in different ways) by ordinary-language philosophy as well as the comedies of remarriage (as described by Cavell in *Pursuits of Happiness*). See, for example, *Themes out of School*, pp. 191–92, and "In Quest of the Ordinary," p. 186.

26. The workman here is also the philosopher, philosophy being characterized by "endless responsibility for one's own discourse, for not resting with words you do not happily mean" (GRK, 35). In this same essay Cavell finds "discourse bearing endless responsibility for itself" in what will seem to many an unlikely place: Coleridge's *Biographia Literaria* (see pp. 52–55). Cavell claims—I think rightly—that the book is "composed entirely without digression."

27. I adapt here a comment from "The Availability of Wittgenstein's Later Philosophy": "If speaking *for* someone else seems to be a mysterious process, that may be because speaking *to* someone does not seem mysterious enough" (MWM, 67–68).

28. On finding, or recovering, your own voice, see "Being Odd, Getting Even," p. 108; "The Melodrama of the Unknown Woman: A Reading of *Gaslight*," p. 27 (where Cavell speaks of "reinserting or replacing the human voice in philosophical thinking, that voice that philosophy finds itself to need to deny, or displace"); and "The Philosopher in American Life," pp. 12–13 (where Cavell argues that logical analysis "has depended upon the suppression of the human voice"—the voice that ordinary-language philosophy aims at recovering).

29. "Consequences," *Critical Inquiry* 11 (March 1985): 443.

30. In "Thinking of Emerson," Cavell makes much the same point: "The answer [to skepticism] does not consist in denying the conclusion of skepticism but in reconceiving its truth. It is true that we do not know the existence of the world with certainty; our relation to its existence is deeper—one in which it is accepted, that is to say, received. My favorite way of putting this is to say that existence is to be acknowledged" (SW, 133).

31. *On Deconstruction*, pp. 229–35.

32. Walter Benn Michaels, "*Walden*'s False Bottoms," in *Glyph*, vol. 1 (Baltimore: Johns Hopkins University Press, 1977), p. 147.

33. Ibid., p. 145.

34. Ibid., p. 147.

35. The predicament in which Michaels's reading leaves us recalls Wordsworth's crisis in book X of *The Prelude:*

Thus I fared
Dragging all passions, notions, shapes of faith,
Like culprits to the bar, suspiciously
Calling the mind to establish in plain day
Her title and her honours, now believing,
Now disbelieving, endlessly perplex'd
With impulse, motive, right and wrong, the ground

> Of moral obligation, what the rule
> And what the sanction, till, demanding *proof,*
> And seeking it in everything, I lost
> All feeling of conviction, and, in fine,
> Sick, wearied out with contrarieties,
> Yielded up moral questions in despair.

Here the demand for proof multiplies the doubts that it is meant to end.

CHAPTER SIX

1. In a July 2, 1984, letter, Cavell describes coming across "uncanny intimacies" between his own work and Derrida's: "Intimate, in a way very little said by my professional colleagues in philosophy is likely to be intimate (I mean among those established; those still looking for themselves are a different matter, one always close to me); and yet abysmally distant, and not just in style."

2. *Writing and Difference,* p. 9.

3. I take this phrase from "Philosophy and the Myth of the Everyday," where Cavell asks, "If the language game is to stop the flow of signification, why are there so many games, so endlessly ramifying?" (PME, 7).

4. Cavell goes on to compare ice in this passage to the frozen seascape of skepticism presented in *The Rime of the Ancient Mariner* (WPC, 24).

5. "Domestic," another one of Cavell's favorite terms (along with "natural"), is also usually used pejoratively in contemporary critical theory. "Domestic life" suggests to some critics boredom and repression and "to domesticate" means to tame or to deprive of power (as when critics deplore the domestication of Derrida's otherwise revolutionary thought). By encouraging us to see more positive possibilities without shying away from these negative ones, Cavell does for "domestic" what he does for "natural."

6. *Wittgenstein and Derrida,* p. 50. See also pp. 52, 63, and 84 for much the same metaphor.

7. Ibid., pp. 85–86.

8. In Cavell's view, Beckett's *Endgame* "portrays a sense of ordinariness denied and, in particular, a sense of extraordinariness captured as ordinary, regarded as ordinary" (IQO, 226). It follows from the surrealism of what we call ordinary that "in order to achieve the ordinary, there is going to have to be an autopsy on what we call the ordinary. As Thoreau saw, we are extraordinary creatures because of what we pick to be ordinary" (IQO, 226). See

also "Ending the Waiting Game," Cavell's essay on *Endgame* in *Must We Mean What We Say?*

9. In this book I have focused on the shortcomings of this critique, not on my considerable sympathy for it. In likening Abrams and Altieri to Austin, I mean to compliment their work as well as to note what I see as its limitations.

INDEX

Abrams, M. H., 17, 156 n.1,
161 n.9; on certainty, 32–34,
100; on Hume and Derrida, 7;
on speech and writing, 105–8,
119–21, 157 n.11
Adams, Hazard, 146 n.14
Alter, Robert, 146 n.14
Altieri, Charles, 7–8, 32, 100,
161 n.9
Aristotle, 12, 15
Austin, J. L.: and Derrida, 8, 32,
151 n.12; as read by Cavell, 23–
24, 34, 125–27, 148 n.22; and
ordinary-language philosophy,
135, 161 n.9

Bacon, Sir Francis, 85
Barzun, Jacques, 36
Bates, Stanley, 143 n.2
Beckett, Samuel, 160 n.8
Benveniste, Emile, 43
Blake, William, 103, 110, 149 n.27,
157 n.13
Bloom, Harold, 38
Booth, Wayne, 17, 36
Bradley, A. C., 36–37
Brooks, Cleanth, 11–12

Cantor, Jay, 7, 143 n.2, 144 n.4
Capra, Frank, 6
Cascardi, A. J., 148 n.23
Cavell, Stanley: as American philosopher, 132–34; on Austin,
23–24, 34, 125–27, 148 n.22; on
comedy of remarriage, 4, 6, 71,
87–94, 118, 133, 139, 158 n.25;
on de Man, 2, 126–30; on
Derrida, 1–2, 132–34, 143 n.1,

160 n.1; on external-world
skepticism, 22–32, 149 nn.24–
25; on farce, 91–92; on Fish,
126–27; on literature and philosophy, 3, 80–81, 153 n.2; on
melodrama, 91–92; on metaphor, 114–16; on ordinary language, 135–38, 152 n.16,
159 nn.27–28, 160 n.8; on
other-minds skepticism, 34–
35, 60–75, 80–81, 140–41; on
skepticism and gender, 31–32,
152 n.19; on Thoreau, 3, 7,
103–4, 108–24, 133–34, 136,
159 nn.22–24, 160 n.8; on
tragedy, 71, 78–79, 80–87, 90–
91, 96–99, 154 n.6, 155 n.12; as
writer, 3, 5
Chaplin, Charlie, 70
Coleridge, Samuel Taylor: *Biographia Literaria*, 3, 159 n.26; and
dejection, 117–18; on literary
form, 36, 38–39, 59–60, 75; *The
Rime of the Ancient Mariner*, 6,
64–65, 111–13, 118, 160 n.4
Comedy, 71, 87–94, 118, 139,
154 n.6
Corngold, Stanley, 24, 99, 151 n.9
Crane, R. S., 12, 14–17
Culler, Jonathan, 6–7, 122,
155 n.14

Danto, Arthur C., 4, 145 n.6
Davidson, Arnold, 144 n.2
Deconstruction and Criticism, 24
de Man, Paul, 140–41, 151 n.9,
158 n.18; on figurative language, 115–16; on grammar

163

Literary criticism

Stanley Cavell's work is distinctive not only in its importance to philosophy but also for its remarkable interdisciplinary range. Cavell is read avidly by students of film, photography, painting, and music, but especially by students of literature, for whom Cavell offers major readings of Thoreau, Emerson, Shakespeare, and others. In this first book-length study of Cavell's writings, Michael Fischer examines Cavell's relevance to the controversies surrounding poststructuralist literary theory, particularly works by Jacques Derrida, J. Hillis Miller, Paul de Man, and Stanley Fish.

Throughout his study, Fischer focuses on skepticism, a central concern of Cavell's multifaceted work. Cavell, following J. L. Austin and Wittgenstein, does not refute the radical epistemological questioning of Descartes, Hume, and others, but rather characterizes skepticism as a significant human possibility or temptation. As presented by Fischer, Cavell's accounts of both external-world and other-minds skepticism share significant affinities with deconstruction, a connection overlooked by contemporary literary theorists.

Fischer follows Cavell's lead in examining how different genres address the problems raised by skepticism and goes on to show how Cavell draws on American and English romanticism in fashioning a response to it. He concludes by analyzing Cavell's remarks about current critical theory, focusing on Cavell's uneasiness with some of the conclusions reached by its practitioners. Fischer shows that Cavell's insights, grounded in powerful analyses of Descartes, Hume, and Wittgenstein, permit a fresh view of Derrida, Miller, de Man, and Fish. The result is not only a revealing characterization of deconstruction but a much-needed and insightful introduction to Cavell's rich but difficult oeuvre.

MICHAEL FISCHER is professor of English at the University of New Mexico. He is the author of *Does Deconstruction Make Any Difference?: Poststructuralism and the Defense of Poetry in Modern Criticism* and coeditor of *Romanticism and Contemporary Criticism*.

Cover photograph by John Rubin.

THE UNIVERSITY OF CHICAGO PRESS

ISBN 0-226-25141-1